**Fodor's**

# GAY GUIDE

## TO THE

*pacific northwest*

BY ANDREW COLLINS

FODOR'S TRAVEL PUBLICATIONS, INC.
NEW YORK • TORONTO • LONDON • SYDNEY • AUCKLAND
HTTP://WWW.FODORS.COM/

# Fodor's Gay Guide to the Pacific Northwest

**Editor:** Daniel Mangin
**Editorial Contributors:** Steven K. Amsterdam, Glen Berger, Kaline J. Carter, Steve Crohn, Janet Foley, James Sinclair
**Map Editor:** Robert P. Blake
**Creative Director:** Fabrizio La Rocca
**Cartographer:** David Lindroth, Inc.; Eureka Cartography
**Cover Design:** Allison Saltzman
**Text Design:** Between the Covers

## Copyright

## Special Sales

# CONTENTS

## Author's Note                                      vii

Eats Price Chart *viii*
Sleeps Price Chart *ix*

---

**1    *Out in* Seattle                                    1**

Eats *10*
Scenes *22*
Sleeps *28*

---

**2    *Out in* the San Juan Islands            34**

Eats *41*
Scenes *47*
Sleeps *47*

---

**3    *Out in* Vancouver                            53**

Eats *64*
Scenes *77*
Sleeps *81*

---

**4    *Out in* Victoria and                           88
       Salt Spring Island**

Eats *98*
Scenes *104*
Sleeps *105*

---

**5    *Out in* Portland                               112**

Eats *121*
Scenes *133*
Sleeps *138*

---

**6    *Out in* Eugene                               142**

Eats *147*
Scenes *150*
Sleeps *151*

**7**    *Elsewhere in*                                    **154**
         *the Pacific Northwest*

         Ashland, Oregon *154*
         Yachats, Oregon *155*
         Tofino, British Columbia *156*
         Whistler, British Columbia *157*

         **Index**                                         **158**

## Maps

The Pacific Northwest *xii*          Greater Vancouver *74–75*
Downtown Seattle *12–13*             Victoria *99*
Greater Seattle *19*                 Salt Spring Island *102*
San Juan Islands                     Downtown Portland
  *44–45*                              *124–125*
Downtown Vancouver                   Greater Portland *128–129*
  *66–67*                            Eugene *148*

# AUTHOR'S NOTE

**B**EING GAY OR LESBIAN influences our choice of accommodations, nightlife, dining, shopping, and perhaps even sightseeing. This book will enable you to plan your trip confidently and with authority. On the following pages I've tried to provide ideas for every segment of our community, giving you the skinny on everything from bars and clubs to gay beaches, from where to buy hiking gear (and cruise the outdoorsy queer customers) on Seattle's Capitol Hill to who serves the best sushi in Vancouver. You'll also find a wide selection of accommodations in every destination, from exclusively lesbian or gay resorts to mainstream hotels.

## About Me

I'm a gay male in my late twenties. I grew up in Connecticut, graduated from Wesleyan University, have lived briefly in London and Atlanta, and currently divide my time between a small house in New Hampshire's Monadnock mountains and an apartment in New York City's East Village.

## How I Researched This Book

I've made several trips to the Pacific Northwest over the past few years; most recently I spent three months driving up and down the West Coast, crashing on friends' sofas and testing out dozens of hotels and guest houses. At every stop I interviewed gays and lesbians—newspaper editors, activists, barflies, and people on the street—to get the latest scoop.

This is an opinionated book. I don't hesitate to say what I think—I'm prone to describe certain neighborhoods as characterless, resorts as touristy or uppity, restaurants as dumpy or over-the-top. My intention is always to relate what I've observed and what I've heard locals say.

For the most part, I travel without announcing myself—the majority of the businesses in this book had no idea I was writing about them when I visited. In the end *Fodor's Gay Guide to the Pacific Northwest* is a service not to hotels and guest houses, or to gay bars and restaurants, or to anybody in the travel industry. It is a resource for you, the traveler.

### Language and Voice

I've written this book in a casual, personal voice, using terms such as "faggy," "dyke," and "queer" the way my friends and I do in general conversation. I know that for some people these words are painful reminders of more repressive times—be assured that no offense is intended. Also, unless the context suggests otherwise, when I use the terms "gay" or "homosexual," I'm referring to gay men and lesbians. I specify gender only as needed for clarity.

## Content

Each chapter is divided into several sections. Here's a quick rundown:

### The Lay of the Land
If you're looking for a quick summation of each destination's geography, its neighborhoods and major attractions, and its shopping, you'll want to read this carefully. At the end are tips on getting around.

### Eats
I'm a restaurant junkie, so I've included a broad range of options. The places I investigated were suggested by gay and lesbian locals, advertise in gay publications, or were reviewed positively in local newspapers and magazines. I stopped by almost every restaurant (and ate at as many as I could) to study the menu, check out the decor and ambience, and observe the crowd.

I've tried to include choices for every budget. Many recommendations are in or near gay-oriented neighborhoods. A few establishments get a nod less for the food than the overtly festive atmosphere. Conversely, some places are listed because they represent some of the destination's finest or most unusual dining. The omission of your personal favorite may be more because it was similar to a place I did review than because I think it's not up to snuff. Unless otherwise noted, any restaurant in this book is at least somewhat popular with the community.

The Eats section ends with a sampling of area coffeehouses. Unless I describe the food, assume that each serves only coffee and light snacks.

The following charts explain the price categories used for restaurants in this guide:

CHART A

| CATEGORY | COST* |
| --- | --- |
| $$$$ | over $20 |
| $$$ | $15–$20 |
| $$ | $9–$14 |
| $ | under $9 |

*cost of dinner entrée*

CHART B

| CATEGORY | COST* |
| --- | --- |
| $$$$ | over $16 |
| $$$ | $12–$16 |
| $$ | $7–$11 |
| $ | under $7 |

*cost of dinner entrée*

CHART C

| CATEGORY | COST* |
| --- | --- |
| $$$$ | over C$23 |
| $$$ | C$17–C$23 |
| $$ | C$11–C$16 |
| $ | under C$11 |

*cost of dinner entrée (Canadian currency)*

## Scenes

I checked out nearly every bar in Eugene, Portland, Seattle, Vancouver, Victoria, and several towns near them. If a place opened after my visit, I telephoned an employee and also got a report from a knowledgeable local resource to ensure an accurate review.

The most popular spots are listed under the heading "Prime Suspects" and are also located with bullets on the dining maps. I've also written short reviews about neighborhood bars, roving parties, and sporadic events—plus a few straight bars with queer-friendly reputations.

Male-oriented places outnumber those that cater to women by about 10 to 1. This is not a reflection of my preferences but of Canadian and U.S. gay-bar culture—it's overwhelmingly young and male. Still, don't assume that a bar described as 80% male or mostly young doesn't welcome lesbians or older guys. Descriptions of each bar's crowd and its "cruise factor" are based on my observations and interviews and are provided simply to give you a profile of what's typical.

Under the heading "Action," I've listed a few bathhouses, adult theaters, and the like. I'd be remiss if I didn't tell you what's where. (I would also be remiss if I didn't encourage you to play safely and observe local regulations.)

## Sleeps

In most chapters I've included any gay-specific establishments that I felt confident recommending. I visited most of the B&Bs and small inns (usually anonymously), though I stayed in only a handful. If the establishment was straight-owned and I had no knowledge of its gay-friendliness, I checked with the owners to verify their interest in being covered in a gay publication. My descriptions of the clientele, compiled without the owners' input, are there to give you a general sense of the place.

When I discuss larger hotels, particularly those in cities, don't assume that they are gay-friendly (or otherwise) unless the reviews specifically state so. Obviously the degree of tolerance you encounter at a large property with many employees will depend largely on who happens to assist you. I included both mainstream properties that are in and near gay neighborhoods and those that have a strong reputation with the community.

The following charts explain the price categories used for lodging establishments in this guide:

CHART A

| CATEGORY | COST* |
|----------|-------|
| $$$$ | over $180 |
| $$$ | $130–$180 |
| $$ | $90–$130 |
| $ | under $90 |

*cost of double-occupancy room in high season

| CHART B | |
| --- | --- |
| CATEGORY | COST* |
| $$$$ | over $150 |
| $$$ | $115–$150 |
| $$ | $75–$115 |
| $ | under $75 |

*cost of double-occupancy room in high season

| CHART C | |
| --- | --- |
| CATEGORY | COST* |
| $$$$ | over C$210 |
| $$$ | C$160–C$210 |
| $$ | C$105–C$160 |
| $ | under C$105 |

*cost of double-occupancy room in high season (Canadian currency)

## The Little Black Book

This is your quick resource guide. If some establishments have closed by the time you read about them—bars and restaurants are unpredictable—try the contacts here to get the latest info. Local tourist boards can be helpful, and lesbigay bookstores and community centers are tremendous resources. I've included a few gay-popular gyms and the phone numbers of resources for persons who are HIV-positive or who have AIDS.

## Crossing the Border

### Identification

U.S. and Canadian citizens must show proof of citizenship and identity to cross the border (a passport, birth certificate with raised seal, or voter registration card is preferred, but a driver's license will usually suffice).

## Currency

The units of currency in Canada are the Canadian dollar (C$) and the cent, in almost the same denominations as in the United States. One- and two-dollar bills are no longer used; they have been replaced by coins. At press time the exchange rate was C$1.35 to US$1.

## Disclaimer

This is where I'm to remind you that time brings changes, and that neither I nor Fodor's can accept responsibility for errors. An incredible amount of time and effort has been spent ensuring the accuracy of this book's information, but businesses move and/or close and restaurants and bars change. Always call an establishment before you go to make sure that it will be open when you get there.

The mention of any business, attraction, or person in this book is in no way an indication of sexual orientation or attitudes about sexual orientation. Unless specifically stated, no business in this book is implied or assumed to be gay-owned or operated.

## Send Letters

Whatever your reaction to this book—delight, excitement, unbridled rage—your feedback is greatly appreciated. I'd love to hear about your experiences, both good and bad, and about establishments you'd like me to include or exclude in future editions. Send your letters to me c/o Fodor's Travel Publications, 201 East 50th Street, New York, NY 10022, or e-mail me at gayfodors@aol.com.

In the meantime, I hope you'll have as much fun using this guide as I had writing it.

*Andrew Collins*

Andrew Collins
February 1997

## Acknowledgments

I've been helped immeasurably by my editor, Daniel Mangin, a senior editor at Fodor's who's better known in the community as a film critic and teacher, a gossip columnist for the *Bay Area Reporter*, and for his gays-in-the-cinema film-clip show *Psycho Killers and Twisted Sisters*. His expertise in the spheres of travel and queer culture are in evidence throughout the book. Also at Fodor's I'd like to thank Glen Berger, a resident of the Pacific Northwest until his recent move to New York, for his input. Many Pacific Northwesterners shared their insights and opinions with me. I'm particularly grateful to the following: Sean Beahen; Bill and Lorcan at the Blue Ewe; Christopher Brandmeir; Allen Braude, Jim Deva, and Janine Fuller at Little Sisters Bookstore; Jim Britten from O' Canada House; Leah Bullard; Margaret Butler; Andrew Caldwell; Dorrie and Helen from Madison, Wisconsin; Cliff Edge and Les Howell; Howard Ehrlich and the late Bill Browning; Rees Erwin; Cindy Filipenko and Pat Johnson at *Xtra West*; Mark Friedman; Peter Goldfarb at the White Swan Inn; Deneen Holler; Peter Johnson; Nathan Kibler; Robert Liberty; Emerson Lim; Janet Murie; Tammy Phillips at Canadian Pacific Hotels; Evan Penner from the West End Guest House; Tony Potter; Rob and Klein from B.J.'s; Eric Rockey and Steve Sickenberger; Susan Solari at the Portland Convention and Visitors Association; Dan Reed; Craig Stroud; Maggie Thompson at the Claddagh House.

# The Pacific Northwest

Clearwater

BRITISH COLUMBIA

Kamloops

Vancouver
Island

Whistler

Kelowna

Tofino
Salt Spring
Island
Nanaimo

Vancouver

New Westminster
Bellingham

Sidney
San Juan
Islands
Anacortes

North
Cascades
National
Park

Coulee
Dam

Victoria

Port
Angeles
Port
Townsend

Whidbey
Island

Olympic
National
Park

Seattle

Bremerton
Tacoma

Olympia
WASHINGTON

90

101
Mt.
Rainier
National
Park

Yakima

Walla
Walla

N

Long Beach

5

82

Columbia River

Portland
84
Pendleton

84

101

Corvallis
Salem

Yachats
Springfield

126

Florence
126
Bend

Eugene

OREGON

Burns

5

101

Crater Lake
National
Park

100 miles

Medford
0

150 km

Ashland

CALIFORNIA

# 1 *Out in Seattle*

**I**T'S AWFULLY DIFFICULT NOT TO LOVE SEATTLE. Of course, most locals want their city to be scorned and ridiculed. Travel guides, it is hoped, will assure the world that the place is overrated and nobody need move here. Well, Seattle is a wonderful city, one that's frequently rated in magazine surveys as being among the most livable on earth. But it's also bursting at the seams, its narrow streets unable to handle additional traffic and its cost of living rising sharply. "If you want to visit, fine," seems to be the attitude of most Seattleites. "But for God's sake, don't move here!"

One common myth is that most migration to Seattle is by way of San Francisco. Ask around, though, and you'll discover that newcomers hail from every corner of America. Why? It used to be that young, often disaffected men and women with a spiritual, environmentalist, or feminist bent moved to San Francisco. This is less true today. Seattle—vibrant and moving forward—has given the Bay Area a run for its money. When considering what to drink, what music to embrace, how to communicate, and how to preserve natural resources, America's twentysomethings take many of their cues from Seattle.

What do Seattleites drink? A funny thing about these folks—they're obsessed with health. They walk, jog, rollerblade, and cycle everywhere they go. They eat wisely. They're early to bed and early to rise. And yet nearly the entire population is addicted to coffee and microbrewed beer. Hmmm. . . .

What kind of music do Seattleites listen to? The heady, harsh alternative sound emanating from the city's hottest clubs is generally labeled grunge, a term that describes not only the style of music but also the deliberately shaggy attire and sensitive, brooding attitude of its aficionados. Local bands such as Nirvana and Pearl Jam were grunge pioneers. Now Seattle has hundreds of budding alternative rockers attempting to carry the torch.

How do Seattleites communicate? They hold referendums. There is always some landmark being slated for demolition or group being threatened by an unfair statute. A recent controversy concerned the possible redevelopment of 400-plus commercial and residential acres stretching from Denny Way to Lake Union. Taxpayers would have footed about one-third of the $300 million tab to reinvent this gloomy neighborhood had the proposal to build Seattle Commons proceeded. Opponents saw the plan as a way for investors and developers to line their pockets by displacing working-class residents. Proponents saw Seattle Commons as a beautification project that would pump money back into the local economy while eradicating urban blight. The conflict pitted egalitarian ideals against the push for progress. Seattle Commons was voted down in 1996.

How else do Seattleites communicate? They surf the Internet. The nearby suburb of Redmond is headquarters to Microsoft, a major engineer of the world's information superhighway. The joke is that everybody in this city either works for Microsoft or is forming a grunge band, if not both. And everybody seems to possess a state-of-the-art computer—it's about as necessary here as owning a phone.

How are Seattleites preserving their natural resources? First, failing to recycle in Seattle is like robbing a bank. A staggering 89% of the population recycles on a regular basis. Laws against pollution are strictly enforced—the waterways surrounding the city are among the cleanest in the United States. People carpool to work whenever possible, or they blade and cycle. City buses even have bike racks and, to encourage people not to drive, are free within downtown.

The greatest concentration of gays is in Capitol Hill, but the district is by no means a ghetto. Students, yuppies, latter-day hippies, and young families all live here, the cutting-edge music, liberal politics, coffeehouses and microbreweries, computer technology, and environmentalism among the ties that bind the area's disparate elements.

In this respect Seattle differs from many U.S. cities, particularly those in the Northeast. And Capitol Hill's demography may offer clues to the ways in which urban neighborhoods are changing vis-à-vis sexual orientation. Capitol Hill does not function as a zone into which gay people retreat to find strength and safety in numbers, but rather as a desirable setting, with great shops, clubs, and restaurants, where people accept one another at face value. Were Seattle as a whole less tolerant, a more insular gay neighborhood might be necessary.

# THE LAY OF THE LAND

Several bodies of water define Seattle's boundaries. To the west is Puget Sound. Off the sound is Elliott Bay, a snug harbor whose shores constitute the western edge of downtown. To the east is Lake Washington. Snaking across the northern half of Seattle is a stretch of water that begins in the west as the Lake Washington Ship Canal, becomes Lake Union, and continues on as Portage Bay and then Union Bay before finally emptying into Lake Washington. From nearly every elevated point in Seattle—and this is a hilly city—water is visible.

The significant chunk of Seattle west of I–5, above the West Seattle Freeway, and below Mercer Street, actually looks urban—with industry and warehouses to the south and downtown's glimmering contemporary skyline to the north. The rest of Seattle is unusually green and almost suburban. Some older, tonier neighborhoods are between downtown and Lake Washington. In northern Seattle, above Lake Union, stretches a vast enclave of relatively young middle-class residents.

## Capitol Hill and Volunteer Park
The western border of **Capitol Hill** begins where I–5 cuts through the city. Prospect Street and Volunteer Park border the neighborhood on the north, 20th Avenue on the east, and Union Street and Seattle University on the south. Due south of Capitol Hill the smaller **First Hill** district contains many medical centers and office buildings.

Capitol Hill has few attractions, but several commercial pockets are excellent for shopping, club hopping, cheap dining, and people-watching. **Pine and Pike streets,** which run east–west, Pine one block north of Pike—don't be upset if you confuse Pine and Pike, even locals do—hold many gay bars, plus some live-music halls and coffeehouses. Also here are few great shops, such as the women's erotica emporium **Toys in Babeland** (⌧ 711 E. Pike St., ☎ 206/ 328–2914) and the thrift and antique clothing store (one of several in this area) **Vintage Voola** (⌧ 705 E. Pike St., ☎ 206/324–2808). For better and worse Seattle has major plans to develop the Pike–Pine corridor—Planet Hollywood has already touched down.

**Broadway Avenue** from Pike about 10 blocks north to Roy Street bustles with a youthful mix of straight and gay-popular businesses. The common denominators are funkiness and thrift, though Broadway is gentrifying as the hippest crowds migrate south toward Pine and Pike. Still, you'll find incredibly cheap food and lots of fun clothing and bric-a-brac. A must-visit is **Broadway Market** (✉ 300 Broadway Ave. E), the largest queer-themed commercial space in America. This three-story atrium mall is loaded with gift shops, stalls, clothing stores, a few restaurants, a gym, a parking garage, and a cinema. The **Pink Zone** (✉ 211 Broadway Ave., ☎ 206/325–0050) recently moved from the Broadway Market into a more visible storefront. This much-talked-about salon-cum-boutique proffers "queer shears and visibly queer gear."

Capitol Hill's other major north–south thoroughfare is **15th Avenue.** From about Madison to Mercer streets it's a tad more upscale and mature than Broadway, with better restaurants, some antiques stores, and **City People's Mercantile** (✉ 500 15th Ave. E, ☎ 206/324–9510), often dubbed Seattle's dyke hardware and household goods emporium.

Rolling, tree-lined streets and an amazingly eclectic selection of houses and apartment buildings—from Victorian painted ladies to '50s Bauhaus-inspired cubes—grace the remainder of Capitol Hill. Fifteenth Avenue rewards you with dramatic views of Elliott Bay; along 23rd Avenue you can see east across Lake Washington.

Gorgeous **Volunteer Park,** easily entered from 14th Avenue or Highland Drive, is home to the exotic-plant-filled **Conservatory** (☎ 206/684–4743) and a 75-foot water tower from which you can enjoy panoramic city views. The **Seattle Asian Art Museum** (✉ 1400 E. Prospect St., ☎ 206/654–3100) has a comprehensive collection. Throngs of queens and lesbians lounge on Volunteer Park's lawns, reading books and each other. At night it can get quite social here (Be warned: It's heavily policed); Seattle, in fact, has an awful lot of cruisy outdoor parks.

## Downtown

America has livelier commercial districts, but downtown Seattle has one remarkable thing going for it: **Pike Place**

**Market** (⊠ Pike St., at 1st Ave., ☏ 206/682−7453). And to think that urban planners during the '60s were ready to tear it down until Seattleites voted to protect the complex as a historic site. The sprawling 1907 structure is abuzz with fishmongers and food marketers of every ilk. Pike Place is on a steep hill; the lower floors hold some genuinely interesting shops, and the ground floor leads under the hideous Highway 99 to the waterfront and its 20 blocks of piers, many of them with restaurants, shops, boat tours, and other attractions. South of Pike Place at Pier 59 is the **Seattle Aquarium** (☏ 206/386−4320). To the north at Pier 66 is the new **Odyssey Contemporary Maritime Museum** (☏ 206/623−2120). The market and the waterfront are touristy, but the area's history and its high-quality shopping and amusements make it worth braving even if you disdain crowds.

The rest of downtown is not particularly memorable. At night the sidewalks are left largely to the homeless and by day it's fairly corporate. One sight worth visiting is the **Seattle Art Museum** (⊠ 100 University St., ☏ 206/654−3100), whose collection emphasizes Asian, Native American, African, and pre-Columbian art. Not everybody loves architect Robert Venturi's postmodern design, but few observers are without a strong opinion.

## Pioneer Square and the International District

Many of the buildings in **Pioneer Square** date from just after 1889, the year a fire destroyed most of the city's wood-frame buildings. Technically part of downtown, these blocks around the intersection of 1st and 2nd avenues and Yesler Way comprised the city's first business district.

In the early years industrialist Henry Yesler operated a sawmill and pier at the foot of what is now Yesler Way. The forests along the hillside provided timber; each tree was cut and rolled down the hill to the mill. The long, muddy, bare incline became known as Skid Road. Eventually, successful commerce moved north and the area became overrun with brothels and saloons; "Skid Row" became forever synonymous with poverty and drunkenness.

After a decline lasting from the Depression until the early 1970s, Pioneer Square was cleaned up, though with mixed success. Buildings were restored and shops and cafés moved in. But many of the older saloons and hangouts, including a couple of long-running if divey gay bars, are still here—as are many Skid Row panhandlers and drunks (try not to trip over the 40-ounce malt-liquor bottles strewn around the cobbled pedestrian malls). At night the square is a mostly collegiate party area; by day it's a good place for wandering through art galleries and the **Downtown Antique Market** (⊠ 2218 Western Ave.), which features 70 dealers.

The garrulous Bill Spiedel conducts a colorful if hokey 90-minute tour called **Underground Seattle** (☎ 206/682–1511) that explores Pioneer Square's original sidewalks and storefronts, many of which still exist intact below ground. After the 1889 fire, city leaders leveled part of Seattle because of an unpleasant waste-disposal problem (the rising tide constantly backed up the sewers). They shaved off several hills and elevated some valleys close to the waterfront. Pioneer Square was raised, its original ground-level sidewalks and stores converted into basements. Beside one of the entrances to the underground is **South End Steam Baths** (⊠ 115½ 1st Ave. S), one of the oldest gay bathhouses on the West Coast.

South of Pioneer Square and east of the massive Seattle Kingdome sports stadium is the century-old, 12-block **International District,** where many Chinese, Japanese, Laotian, Thai, Vietnamese, and Filipino immigrants live and work. Chinese workers hired to complete the transcontinental railroad first settled here, and despite anti-Chinese riots in the 1880s and the internment of Japanese Americans during World War II, the neighborhood has continued to thrive. A highlight is **Uwajimaya** (⊠ 519 6th Ave. S, ☎ 206/624–6248), an immense Japanese department store with an exotic-foods section.

## Belltown
North of downtown and bounded by Stewart Street to the south, 6th Avenue to the east, Battery Street to the north, and the waterfront to the west, is **Belltown,** a commercial and residential haven of artists, musicians, and bookish yuppies. You'll find great antiques and thrift shops, galleries, restaurants, and some of the city's hottest music clubs—the highest concentrations are along 1st and 2nd avenues.

## Seattle Center and Queen Anne Hill
Due north of Belltown above Denny Way is the working-class neighborhood that would have been **Seattle Commons** had voters approved that plan. Private developers continue to work

on reinventing the area, which contains some rock clubs, several photography and film studios, and **REI** (⊠ 222 Yale Ave. N, ☎ 206/223–1944), where outdoorsy types arm themselves with tents, bikes, hiking boots, and Swiss Army knives.

Northwest of Belltown is **Seattle Center,** the 74-acre tract that hosted the 1962 World's Fair. The center may have piqued architectural curiosity 30 years ago, but today it provides an embarrassing glimpse into '60s planners' notions of ultramodernity. The highlight of this kooky spot is the **Space Needle** (⊠ 5th and Broad Sts., ☎ 206/443–2111) the retrofuturist 600-foot tower visible from most anywhere in the city. You can take an elevator to the top for great vista (forget the restaurant, it's relentlessly mediocre). The best thing about the view from the Space Needle is that you can't see the Space Needle. Two high-profile theater groups, the **Seattle Rep** and **Intiman,** perform at Seattle Center, as does the city's highly regarded ballet troupe. Also here is the **Pacific Science Center** (⊠ 200 2nd Ave. N, ☎ 206/443–2880), which contains touch-friendly exhibits.

Just west of Seattle Center you can head up steep Queen Anne Avenue to **Queen Anne Hill,** a stately historic neighborhood of restored houses and fun stores, coffeehouses, and pubs that sits 457 feet above Elliott Bay. Lots of yuppies—straight and gay—live here; most of the action is on the lower part of the hill.

## The Lake Washington Shoreline

Many visitors neglect the east side of Seattle, which includes the well-to-do enclaves of **Madison Valley** and **Madison Park.** It's worth driving or cycling through the rolling hills of these bucolic neighborhoods that overlook scenic Lake Washington.

From downtown head east on Yesler Way to **Lake Washington Boulevard,** which skirts the lake's shoreline. Go north a half mile or so to reach **Denny-Blaine Park** (a.k.a. Dyke-kiki, as in Waikiki), a neat but compact lakeside lawn. This is the city's unofficial lesbian tanning salon. There are two levels; if you wish to go topless, head to the lower one, which has access to some great swimming. From this park you can see the homes of two local icons: Behind you, on Lake Washington Boulevard, is the home of the late Kurt Cobain—his widow, Courtney Love, and their daughter, Frances Bean, still reside here. Across the lake you can see the sprawling construction project that someday (it's taking years to build) will be the palace of billionaire computer whiz Bill Gates, chairman of Microsoft.

Continue north on Lake Washington Boulevard to Madison Street. A right turn leads down the hill to **Madison Park,** a long sandy beach overlooking the lake. North of the lifeguard station the crowd is mostly gay. There's a float out in the water that on hot summer days looks like an ad for Speedo swimsuits. Madison Street and the blocks just off it have good shops and gay-popular restaurants, including **Cactus** (*see* Eats, *below*) and **Mangoes Thai Cuisine** (✉ 1841 42nd Ave. E, ☎ 206/324–6467).

Take Madison Street back up to Lake Washington Boulevard, hang a right, and follow it to the **University of Washington Park Arboretum** (✉ 2300 Arboretum Dr. E, ☎ 206/543–8800), a shady public expanse containing more than 5,000 varieties of plants and many winding trails. If you continue to where Lake Washington Boulevard passes by the on-ramp to I–520, you can park at the nearby lot and follow the path to find the city's fave cruise grounds. Plenty of people wander through here just to enjoy the scenery and nonhuman wildlife as well.

## The University District, Wallingford, and Fremont

Take I–5 over Lake Union to the Northeast 45th Street exit to reach several personable, untouristy northern Seattle communities, including the University District, Wallingford, and Fremont.

Heading east on 45th Street leads to the **University of Washington's** beautiful, hilly campus. The U. District isn't gay, but it's full of quirky diversions, cheap eats, and vintage clothing stores, especially along the neighborhood's main drag, **University Way.**

From I–5 follow Northeast 45th Street west several blocks to its intersection with **Meridian Avenue.** This is the heart of Seattle's most significant lesbian community, low-key **Wallingford.** Stop by the **Wallingford Center** (✉ 4430 Wallingford Ave. N), a small indoor shopping complex. If you need a bite to eat, or just want to meet a few local lezzies, check out **Julia's** (*see* Eats, *below*), a bright little café and juice bar.

Continue west on Northeast 45th Street to Fremont Avenue, then turn left to reach **Fremont,** which is just north of Queen Anne Hill across the Lake Washington Ship Canal. Seattle's hippie haven of the 1960s today hosts a mix of grungers and yuppies. As you enter the neighborhood via the Fremont Bridge, a sign welcomes you to "The Center of the Universe." For some relatively funky window-shopping, check out the intersection of 35th Street and Fremont Avenue. Sweet tooths should definitely stop by **Simply Desserts** (⊠ 3421 Fremont Ave. N, ☎ 206/633–2671), where confections such as a chocolate-cognac torte await. On Sundays vendors show crafts, antiques, and objets d'art at the **Fremont Market,** a two-block plot just off Fremont Avenue.

Head north of Fremont and Wallingford on Highway 99 to get to **Woodland Park** and **Green Lake.** The **Woodland Park Zoo** (⊠ 5500 Phinney Ave. N, ☎ 206/684–4800) is one of the best in the nation at creating authentic animal habitats. The Seattle Rose Garden is also inside the park. An emerald trace of lawns and leafy trees fringes Green Lake; shells, rowboats, and swimmers compete for space on the water, while walkers, bladers, and cyclists enjoy the grounds. Lesbians maintain a high visibility throughout this area.

# GETTING AROUND

You enter Seattle by way of I–5 from the north or south, or I–90 from the east or west. You can definitely get around the city without a car, especially downtown and on Capitol Hill. If you're here for more than a few days, however, consider renting a car to see some of the outer neighborhoods. Traffic is a drag: Seattle's dated network of streets is ill-equipped to handle the volume. **Metro Transit** (☎ 206/553–3000 or 800/542–7876) buses are fairly practical for getting around even the more remote neighborhoods, and they're free within downtown. It's possible to hail a taxi on the street, but it's best to phone—**Graytop Cab** (☎ 206/622–4800) is one option—or, if you're near a downtown hotel get in line at its cabstand.

The **Seattle-Tacoma International Airport,** known as Sea-Tac, is 30 minutes south of downtown on I–5. Taxis cost about $25. **Gray Line Airport Express** (☎ 206/626–6088) service to downtown hotels costs $7.50. Pickups are outside the international and United Airlines baggage claim areas. **Shuttle Express** (☎ 206/622–1424; in Washington, 800/487–7433) has 24-hour door-to-door service for $18. **Metro Transit** (☎ 206/553–3000 or 800/542–7876) city buses (Express Tunnel Bus 194 and regular Buses 174 and 184) pick up passengers outside the baggage claim areas.

# WHEN TO GO

Seattle has very distinct high and low seasons. The weather is relatively mild year-round, but you'll have an easier time finding a room in the winter, when Seattle can be fairly gray and wet. The sunny cool summer brings hordes of travelers; the city's seeming wealth of hotel rooms dwindles, and reservations at least six weeks in advance are a must.

Seattle's **pride festivities** are extensive and usually held in late June. The **Seattle International Film Festival** (☎ 206/325–6825) takes place over three weeks in late May and early June and always presents a number of lesbian and gay features.

# EATS

Seattle is an easy place to eat well and cheap. Washington, like Oregon and northern California, has fertile soil, a moderate climate, and good farming just about year-round. This means that chefs have continual access to fresh produce. With all the water you can count on plenty of seafood. And then there are the many specialty food shops in the International District. The result is an abundance of Asian-influenced regional cooking that's a major segment of what's come to be known as Pacific Northwest cuisine (which also includes indigenous game and seafood preparations). Authentic Chinese, Thai, and Japanese restaurants are also easy to find.

Most of the pricey restaurants are downtown. Everywhere else, especially on Capitol Hill and in the University District, cheap and filling burritos, sushi, veggie platters, pizzas, and *pad thai,* the popular panfried rice-noodle dish, are readily available.

For price ranges, *see* Chart A at the front of this guide.

# Downtown and Environs

**$$$** ✕ **Campagne.** Very chichi but not overdone, the French restaurant at the Inn at the Market is a terrific place to celebrate your long-term romance or kick off a new one. The country-French specialties (often game) include a starter of seafood sausage and a cinnamon-roasted quail in a carrot-and-orange sauce. An outdoor dining area overlooks Elliott Bay. Downstairs, Cafe Campagne serves more affordable bistro fare (great rotisserie chickens) in a casual atmosphere. ⊠ *86 Pine St.,* ☎ *206/728–2800.*

**$$$** ✕ **El Gaucho.** Belltown's latest culinary venture shuns the overwrought nouvelle cuisine that's all the rage in favor of more traditional Northwest fare—28-day dry-aged Angus beef, baby back ribs, flaming shish kebabs, and bouillabaisse. Light eaters may want to dine elsewhere, though vegetarians will discover a satisfying risotto with wild mushrooms. A baby grand piano and the open kitchen help create the right mood for conversation. ⊠ *2505 1st Ave.,* ☎ *206/728–1337.*

**$$$** ✕ **Queen City Grill.** This Belltown fixture has been converted from an old-fashioned saloon into an elegant wine bar and seafood bistro. The dining room glows with polished wood and black lacquer, and tables have simple white linen. It's a good spot to try out Seattle's exquisite raw oysters on the half shell. Or start with clams sautéed with tomatoes, garlic, and vermouth. Lots of daily fresh-fish specials, too. ⊠ *2201 1st Ave.,* ☎ *206/443–0975.*

**$$–$$$** ✕ **Al Boccolino.** Though it's not always credited as being among the city's top eateries, Al Boccolino serves stellar Italian food. Rigatoni with Gorgonzola and roasted quail wrapped in prosciutto are among the offerings. The romantic triangular dining room has exposed brick, soft lighting, and high ceilings. ⊠ *1 Yesler Way,* ☎ *206/622–7688.*

**$$–$$$** ✕ **b. figueroa.** Chef Barbara Figueroa has been wowing Seattle for years with her fine cooking at other restaurants; recently she opened her own space in a converted brick warehouse amid a strip of trendy home-furnishing shops near Pike Place. Tantalizing dishes include the pan-roasted salmon with chanterelle sauce, black currants, tarragon, and morels, and the seared Muscovy duck with rosemary bread pudding and apple-brandy sauce. ⊠ *1010 Western Ave.,* ☎ *206/682–5799.*

**$$–$$$** ✕ **Dahlia Lounge.** Tom Douglas, an early proponent of Pacific Northwest cuisine, oversees the kitchen at this trendy north-of-downtown restaurant that's decorated with exotic-

12

**Eats** ●

Al Boccolino, **14**

b. figueroa, **12**

B & O Espresso, **22**

Bauhaus Books and Coffee, **19**

Book and Bean Espresso, **23**

Broadway New American Grill, **27**

Cafe Paradiso, **33**

Café Septième, **29**

Campagne, **10**

Coastal Kitchen, **37**

The Crocodile, **4**

Dahlia Lounge, **8**

Dick's Drive-In Restaurant, **30**

The Easy, **32**

El Gaucho, **1**

Elysian Brewing Co., **35**

Flying Fish, **3**

Georgina's, **40**

Glo's, **21**

Good Chow, **2**

Gravity Bar, **7, 26**

Hamburger Mary's, **20**

Hopscotch, **39**

Hopvine Pub, **36**

Jack's Bistro, **38**

Kitto, **24**

Machiavelli, **18**

Noodle Studio, **28**

Painted Table, **13**

The Palace, **6**

Queen City Grill, **5**

Rosebud Espresso, **31**

Siam on Broadway, **25**

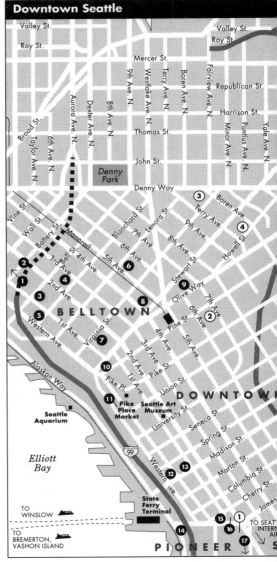

Downtown Seattle

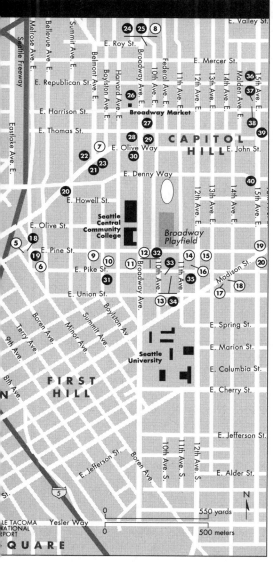

Torrefazione,
**9, 17**
Trattoria
Mitchelli, **15**
Wild Ginger, **11**
Wildrose, **34**
Zasu, **16**

**Scenes** ○

C.C.
Attle's, **20**
The Cuff, **15**
Double Header, **1**
Eagle, **6**
The Easy, **12**
Elite, **8**
Elite II, **7**
Encore, **14**
Kid Mohair, **5**
Madison Pub, **17**
Mr.
Paddywack's, **10**
Neighbours, **11**
R Place, **9**
Re-bar, **4**
Sea Wolf
Saloon, **18**
Sonya's, **2**
Spags, **16**
Thumpers, **19**
Timberline
Tavern, **3**
Wildrose, **13**

fish sculpture. The eclectic menu changes often but might include rabbit grilled with roasted garlic or Asian-inspired lobster-and-shiitake-mushroom pot stickers. Outstanding desserts. ⊠ *1904 4th Ave.,* ☎ *206/682–4142.*

**\$\$–\$\$\$** ✕ **Flying Fish.** The extensive menu of this contemporary fish house lists small plates, large plates, and platters for sharing. Your party can order mussels with a chili-lime dipping sauce for \$7.95 per pound. Or you can try a big dish of crab ravioli with a lemongrass cream sauce. The preparations are unusual, the seafood is always fresh, and the orange-and-yellow dining room is festive and chic. ⊠ *2234 1st Ave.,* ☎ *206/ 728–8595.*

**\$\$–\$\$\$** ✕ **Painted Table.** The reasonable prices at this downtown restaurant are surprising given its location inside one of the city's fanciest hotels. Chef Tim Kelley does wonders with Pacific Northwest fare, including such subtly inventive dishes as herb-crusted lamb with grilled Japanese eggplant, fennel, and polenta. The art-filled bi-level dining room brings out the vibrant colors of Kelley's creations. ⊠ *Alexis Hotel, 1007 1st Ave.,* ☎ *206/624–3646.*

**\$\$–\$\$\$** ✕ **The Palace.** The retrochic neon sign may recall a '50s steak house, but the food is strictly au courant at revolutionary restaurateur Tom Douglas's latest venture. There's always a special such as grilled goat cheese with curried sweet potatoes and coriander chutney. You might also feast on a sampling of starters, most of which are priced affordably (the duck empanada is just \$4). With its soaring wooden columns and royal-blue and gold curtains, the vaulted, two-story dining room is appropriately dramatic. ⊠ *2030 5th Ave.,* ☎ *206/ 448–2001.*

**\$\$–\$\$\$** **Wild Ginger.** Every critic's short list of top Seattle restaurants includes this sophisticated pan-Asian eatery tucked below Pike Place Market. Seating is in an airy open dining room with high ceilings and Asian art. Among the fine menu selections are tuna *manada* (yellowfin tuna wok-fried in a spicy Indonesian candlenut sauce with lemongrass and coconut flakes) and *toi shan* sea scallops (cooked with carrots, pea pods, straw mushrooms, and oyster sauce). The satay bar is open till 2 AM. ⊠ *1400 Western Ave.,* ☎ *206/623–4450.*

**\$\$** ✕ **Zasu.** This offbeat option near Pioneer Square is a sleek haunt with dancing most nights. The kitchen serves up diverse, mostly European dishes, from traditional Welsh rarebit to a zesty Hungarian goulash. ⊠ *608 1st Ave.,* ☎ *206/682–1200.*

**$-$$** ✕ **Good Chow.** Less bohemian than other Belltown places, this perky café has an airy brick courtyard and a staff that's variously perky and airy too. Best bets from the regional menu are the crab sandwich, the greens with crumbled Gorgonzola, and the grilled veggie sandwiches. ⊠ *2331 2nd Ave.,* ☎ *206/443–5833.*

**$** ✕ **The Crocodile.** The restaurant that's part of one of the country's hottest grunge clubs often gets overlooked. True, it's nothing fancy—just a cavernous pseudo diner with big plate-glass windows and a high ceiling—but the pastas, sandwiches, and eggs are excellent. At lunchtime it's actually very relaxed here. ⊠ *2200 2nd Ave.,* ☎ *206/441–5611.*

**$** ✕ **Trattoria Mitchelli.** This sprawling pubby Italian restaurant off Pioneer Square has great sidewalk seating along Yesler Way, hearty pasta dishes (try the black-bean ravioli), and a huge list of microbeers. A bit touristy and noisy, it's open most nights till 4 AM. ⊠ *84 Yesler Way,* ☎ *206/623–3883.*

## Capitol Hill

**$$** ✕ **Broadway New American Grill.** Uneven but reasonably priced American fare marks this major late-night dining option. Some dishes have a nouvelle twist (hence the "New" in "New American") and range from grilled ahi sandwiches to a tasty crab-and-artichoke dip. ⊠ *314 Broadway Ave. E,* ☎ *206/328–7000.*

**$$** ✕ **Coastal Kitchen.** Laughing, chattering groups are almost always in residence at this bright, white-tiled dining room. The cuisine is eclectic, from the rock-shrimp-and-crab cakes to a Caribbean seafood grill to pasta *puttanesca* (tomatoes, garlic, capers, black olives, and anchovies). ⊠ *429 15th Ave. E,* ☎ *206/322–1145.*

**$$** ✕ **Elysian Brewing Co.** This two-level relative newcomer to Capitol Hill draws a huge crowd of twenty- and thirtysomethings—gayfolk from guppies to drag queens to leather daddies, along with many straights. Vegetarian specialties include fajitas and chili, or you can order inexpensive tapas to go with the fine brews. The bar gets hopping later at night when the music starts playing. ⊠ *1221 E. Pike St.,* ☎ *206/ 860–1920.*

**$$** ✕ **Machiavelli.** Set in a large dining room with lots of windows and cheerful red chairs, this poor-man's chic bistro serves decent Italian favorites at reasonable prices. Try the penne with red-pepper pesto, the anchovy pizza, or the eggplant parmigiana. ⊠ *1215 Pine St.,* ☎ *206/621–7941.*

**$$** ✕ **Noodle Studio.** This recent addition to Broadway's string of great ethnic eateries prepares authentic dishes not found in many Seattle Thai restaurants, such as bananas fried in a rice-flour batter and served with shredded coconut and sesame seeds. Barbecued pork with egg noodles is another favorite off an extremely long menu. ⊠ *209 Broadway Ave. E,* ☎ *206/325–6277.*

**$–$$** ✕ **The Easy.** Restaurants attached to gay bars are rarely as good as the dykey Easy. The varied, affordable food includes a fine Caesar salad with a roasted-garlic-and-anchovy dressing, a smoked-chicken-and-brie baguette, and rigatoni Siciliano (with calamata olives, capers, fresh tomatoes, fresh herbs, and garlic with red wine). ⊠ *916 E. Pike St.,* ☎ *206/ 323–8343.*

**$–$$** **Hopscotch.** You'll know you're here when you see the 6-foot-high murals of Scotch-bottle labels outside. The theme continues inside with an extensive collection of Scottish artwork, maps, and flags, plus hand-painted walls depicting hop fields. Completely constructed from red oak, except for the mahogany bar, Hopscotch has a tasty but inexpensive menu—oven-roasted chicken with garlic mashed potatoes, ginger-marinated salmon in steamed rice, and the like. Crab nachos and pan-fried calamari are among the standout appetizers. The bar serves more than 100 single malts. A bagpipe musician plays on weekends. ⊠ *332 15th Ave. E,* ☎ *206/322–4191.*

**$–$$** ✕ **Hopvine Pub.** The ambience here—muted lighting and royal-blue bar stools—is along the lines of a contemporary art gallery; only the wooden booths impart a taverny feel. The young and trendy crowd comes here as much to hear good live music as to sample Seattle-style clam chowder, pesto pizza, thick grinders, and a wide selection of microbeers. ⊠ *507 15th Ave. E,* ☎ *206/328–3120.*

**$–$$** ✕ **Jack's Bistro.** Patrons of this peppy Tuscan- and Provençal-inspired restaurant dine in a sunny courtyard, on the sidewalk, or in a cozy storefront eating area. The menu has fine salads and pastas, and interesting starters such as Gorgonzola polenta. Friendly, low-key staff. Live jazz some nights. ⊠ *405 15th Ave. E,* ☎ *206/324–9625.*

**$–$$** ✕ **Siam on Broadway.** This is easily the best Thai restaurant on the Hill, despite some pretty strong competition. The nightly crowds attest to the great food and service. The *tom* *kah gai* (a peppery chicken, lemongrass, and coconut milk soup) and the spicy vegetable curry dishes are among the best options. ⊠ *616 Broadway Ave. E,* ☎ *206/324–0892.*

**$** ✕ **Dick's Drive-In Restaurant.** The garish orange sign of this renowned burger joint is probably visible from the space shuttle. A '60s-kitsch relic, it's usually packed late at night with hungry grungers and drunk guys. The menu is simple: quarter-pound all-beef patties, plus fries and old-fashioned ice cream. There's a cruisy outdoor counter by the take-out window. ⊠ *115 Broadway Ave. E,* ☎ *206/323–1300. No credit cards.*

**$** ✕ **Giorgina's.** One of the classiest but most casual Italian restaurants on the hill has been lesbian-owned and gay-frequented for years. The softly lit contemporary dining room is always aglow with smiling patrons sampling designer pizzas (garlic clam is a favorite) and light pasta dishes. ⊠ *131 15th Ave. E,* ☎ *206/329–8118.*

**$** ✕ **Glo's.** As opposed to the city's zillion hip coffeehouses, Glo's is a real no-frills coffee shop, open from 7 AM to 3 PM and *the* breakfast choice among dykes and fags. Eggs Benedict, Belgian waffles, and bagels and lox should help start your day. ⊠ *1621 E. Olive Way,* ☎ *206/324–2577. No credit cards.*

**$** ✕ **Gravity Bar.** The postindustrial juice bar on the ground floor of the ultrafaggy Broadway Market is a magnet for cute lesbians. Salads, open-face sandwiches, chapati-bread roll-ups, and rice-and-veggie platters are served under massive chrome air ducts and pipes. And that wheat-grass juice is dee-licious . . . just like Mom's. ⊠ *415 Broadway E,* ☎ *206/325–7186; also in Belltown:* ⊠ *113 Virginia St.,* ☎ *206/448–8826. No credit cards.*

**$** ✕ **Hamburger Mary's.** The fag-happy restaurant chain's Seattle edition looks like a giant fern bar. Tasty burgers and fries are the main offerings, but you might stop in for a late-night banana split. ⊠ *1525 E. Olive Way,* ☎ *206/324–8112.*

**$** ✕ **Kitto.** This Japanese noodle house is probably the best on Capitol Hill, with a wide selection of cooked delicacies. The $4.95 lunch special is a bargain. ⊠ *614 Broadway Ave. E,* ☎ *206/325–8486.*

**$** ✕ **Wildrose.** Like the Easy, Seattle's other lesbian bar, the Wildrose also has a pretty good kitchen. Salads, polenta, and sandwiches on fresh-baked bread are typical fare. The crowd is largely women, but gay men and a few straights have been known to dine in this festive tavern. ⊠ *1021 E. Pike St.,* ☎ *206/324–9210.*

## Elsewhere

$$$–   ✕ **Rover's.** For a special occasion or if you'd just like to taste
$$$$   some of the city's finest country-French fare, make a reservation at this phenomenal restaurant inside a yellow clapboard bungalow off a quiet Madison Valley courtyard. Excellent choices include seared foie gras with rhubarb confit, and an entrée of sautéed venison medallions with wild mushrooms, flageolet beans, and a black peppercorn sauce. ⊠ *2808 E. Madison St.,* ☎ *206/325–7442.*

$$$   ✕ **Kaspar's.** Many epicureans call chef-owner Kaspar Donier a genius. Sample his Alaskan king salmon in a potato crust, Dungeness crab sushi rolls, and grilled free-range chicken with grapes and rosemary and decide for yourself. And check out the excellent wine list. The restaurant is one block west of Key Arena in Seattle Center. ⊠ *19 W. Harrison St.,* ☎ *206/298–0123.*

$$$   ✕ **Ponti Seafood Grill.** Locals love this nouvelle seafood restaurant just across the Lake Washington Ship Canal from Fremont. You can feast on Asian- and Mediterranean-inspired food either in the classy dining rooms or out on a patio. A typical dish: Thai-curry penne with scallops and crab in a ginger-tomato chutney. ⊠ *3014 3rd Ave. N,* ☎ *206/284–3000.*

$$–$$$   ✕ **Cafe Lago.** The specialties at this underrated Montlake (not far from Madison Valley) trattoria are handmade pasta and wood-fired pizzas. A magnificent antipasti selection includes roasted garlic, cured meats, and robust cheeses. ⊠ *2305 24th Ave. E,* ☎ *206/329–8005.*

$$   ✕ **Bandoleone.** Oxblood walls, intimate seating arrangements, installations by local artists, and Latin music draw many repeat customers to this very sexy space where the margaritas are made with fresh-squeezed fruit juices. Signature dishes include chicken stuffed with herb goat cheese and pistachio-crusted Chilean sea bass. Many people stick to the tapas—shrimp and corn cakes are among the favorites. ⊠ *2241 Eastlake Ave. E,* ☎ *206/329–7559.*

$$   ✕ **Bizzarro Cafe.** Looking something like a tornado hit it, this Wallingford trattoria lives up to its name with peculiar bric-a-brac strewn everywhere. But you'll get a lot of dependable traditional Italian food for your money. The mix-and-match

**Eats** ●

5 Spot Cafe, **10**

Bandoleone, **9**

Bizzarro Cafe, **2**

Cactus, **13**

Cafe Flora, **15**

Cafe Lago, **12**

Julia's, **3**

Kaspar's, **11**

Mae's Phinney
Ridge Cafe, **1**

Maple Leaf
Grill, **5**

Philadelphia
Fevre, **16**

Ponti Seafood
Grill, **8**

Rover's, **14**

Simpatico
Bistro, **4**

Still Life, **7**

Union Bay
Cafe, **6**

**Scenes** ○

Changes, **1**

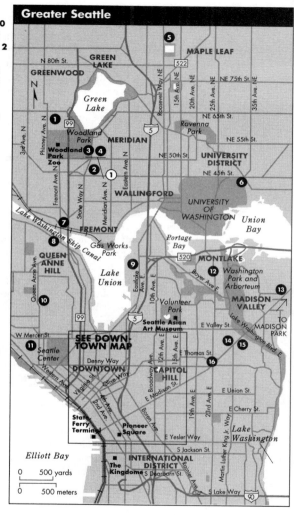

pasta and sauce option is always a smart way to go. ⊠ *1307 N. 46th St.,* ☎ *206/545–7327.*

**$$** ✕ **Cafe Flora.** The most inventive vegetarian restaurant in the city, on the edge of Capitol Hill, welcomes plenty of power dykes and guppies. Munch in the handsome contemporary dining room on such veggie vittles as Oaxaca tacos with spicy mashed potatoes, diced peppers, cheddar and smoked-mozzarella cheeses, and a side of black-bean stew; an Indian chickpea stew; or an apple-jalapeño-chutney quesadilla appetizer. ⊠ *2901 E. Madison St.,* ☎ *206/325–9100.*

**$$** ✕ **5 Spot Cafe.** The emphasis at this venerable neighborhood eatery, two doors from Queen Anne Hill's westernmost radio tower, is on New Orleans fare (great crawfish). But the menu borrows from across the country, with nods to New England, New Mexico, Texas, and the Northwest. The success of these dishes varies, but the atmosphere is fun and bustling. ⊠ *1502 Queen Anne Ave. N,* ☎ *206/285–7768.*

**$$** ✕ **Maple Leaf Grill.** Proof that queers live, eat, and socialize all over town, this neighborhood tavern in northern Seattle lures a mix of gays and straights, young and old. Sprinkled in with the ordinary comfort food are more sophisticated dishes—the chef describes the fare as "down-home postmodern." ⊠ *8909 Roosevelt Way NE,* ☎ *206/523–8449.*

**$$** ✕ **Simpatico Bistro.** For a nice dinner near the University of Washington, this gay-popular Wallingford restaurant never fails. There are booths and tables inside, and also a shaded arborlike patio. The food is Italian: Try lamb shank braised in Chianti with garlic and allspice, or the tangy goat-cheese polenta. ⊠ *4430 Wallingford Ave. N,* ☎ *206/632–1000.*

**$$** ✕ **Union Bay Cafe.** For several years this Laurelhurst bistro northeast of the University District has attracted hungry folks from all over Seattle—including quite a few from the gay community. Chef Mark Manley presents diverse and interesting Pacific Northwest cuisine, with an emphasis on local seafood, free-range poultry, and organic produce. Great wine list, too. ⊠ *3505 N.E. 45th St.,* ☎ *206/527–8364.*

**$–$$** ✕ **Cactus.** This funky but not tacky Mexican restaurant near gay Madison Park Beach is a popular getaway after all that sunning, swimming, and scoping. The food is slightly contemporary, with dishes like papaya-and-avocado salad. There's a substantial tapas menu. ⊠ *4220 E. Madison St.,* ☎ *206/324–4140.*

**$** ✕ **Julia's.** This family restaurant in Wallingford redefines the genre: Yes, straight parents and their kids eat here, but joining them are gay couples (frequently with kids of their own), and folks who just consider each other family. The food is healthful and simple, with pasta, veggie dishes, burgers, baked breads, and fresh salads. There's also a juice bar. The breakfasts here, a daily habit for many, are hearty and delicious. ⊠ *4401 Wallingford Ave.,* ☎ *206/633–1175.*

**$** ✕ **Mae's Phinney Ridge Cafe.** Dykes with tykes, alternateens, yuppies—all these and more weekend brunch at this colorful café in the increasingly queer neighborhood of Greenwood, just north of Woodland Park. Holstein cow art abounds, both inside and on the building's exterior. Not surprisingly, dairy products are heavily featured—this place has the best milk shakes in town. Breakfasts are huge, with memorable cinnamon rolls. You can grab cappuccino in the Mud Room espresso bar. ⊠ *6412 Phinney Ave. N,* ☎ *206/782–1222.*

**$** ✕ **Philadelphia Fevre.** If you've a hankering for such Philly favorites as hoagies (subs or heros to most Americans), cheesesteaks, or scrapple, this casual Madison Valley luncheonette will definitely do the trick. ⊠ *2332 E. Madison St.,* ☎ *206/323–1000. No credit cards.*

**$** ✕ **Still Life.** One of the best cafés in town has an airy seating area with yard-sale-quality wooden tables and chairs. The menu at the Fremont eatery is substantial, with corn-tortilla pie, smoked-salmon bagels, and heavenly hazelnut shortbread. ⊠ *705 N. 35th St.,* ☎ *206/547–9850. No credit cards.*

## Coffeehouse Culture

Seattle is caffeine central. It's where the ever-expanding Starbucks chain originated in 1970—there seems to be a coffeehouse on every corner. If you're still having trouble finding a cup of the jitters, look for one of the more than 200 licensed espresso carts roaming the city streets.

**B & O Espresso.** A fairly bookish and mellow gay crowd—lots of folks chipping away at dog-eared dime novels—hangs out at this Capitol Hill institution. ⊠ *204 Belmont Ave. E,* ☎ *206/322–5028.*

**Bauhaus Books and Coffee.** This java joint on lower Capitol Hill has stacks of art and architecture books and a stylish decor outlined by black wrought-iron grillwork. ⊠ *301 E. Pine St.,* ☎ *206/625–1600.*

**Book & Bean Espresso.** Cerebral sorts pore over the scads of used books at this place with all the usual beans. ⊠ *1635½ E. Olive Way,* ☎ *206/325–1139.*

**Cafe Paradiso.** What's perhaps the gayest coffeehouse in the city is close to its two lesbian bars. Big windows overlook the action on Pike Street. The crowd is more grunge than guppie but there's plenty of each. ⊠ *1005 E. Pike St.,* ☎ *206/322–6960.*

**Café Septième.** You can munch on great sandwiches at this huge, dark, intentionally run-down-looking place that's popular with alternateens. ⊠ *214 Broadway Ave. E,* ☎ *206/860–8858.*

**Rosebud Espresso.** Cozy and crunchy Rosebud has real food (pastas, overstuffed sandwiches), good live jazz many nights, and a whimsical decor of mismatched chairs and tables, sofas, and cushy wing chairs. There's a patio out back. ⊠ *719 E. Pike St.,* ☎ *206/323–6636.*

**Torrefazione.** The Pioneer Square location of this regional chain isn't nearly as gay as the Belltown one, but it has more character, with sidewalk seating along a pedestrian-only cobblestone street of galleries. ⊠ *320 Occidental Ave. S,* ☎ *206/624–5847;* ⊠ *622 Olive Way,* ☎ *206/624–1429.*

# SCENES

If Kate Moss is the sort of girl (or boy) you fancy, you'll love Seattle, whose population of gaunt, waiflike, morose-looking young people is likely the highest of any city in the world (or at least in a developed nation). Transplanted Californians and their love of gyms and tanning salons have made for more buffed-and-bronzed types in recent years, however. At a couple of clubs you'll see guys ripping off their shirts and vogueing, but for the most part Seattleites dress down and behave modestly.

Bar goers are surprisingly mellow and polite—even standing single file for drinks—which imparts an oddly formal air to such a countercultural community. When you finally do reach the bar, you'll be presented with a dizzying variety of microbeers. If you're new to this racket, ask the bartender for a recommendation—or use your ignorance of local brews as a way to inflate the ego of the cute, hopefully knowledgeable creature standing next to you.

A tip for lesbians: During the **University of Washington** women's basketball season (☎ 206/543–2200 for tickets), which runs from November through March, try to take in a game. These events are a big deal among Seattle dykes: Attendance averages more than 3,000—better than any lesbian bar in America! UW has a strong lesbian presence and, you might say, tradition: It's the alma mater of Gertrude Stein's companion, Alice B. Toklas, whose father ran a shop in Seattle.

## Bars and Clubs

PRIME SUSPECTS

**C.C. Attle's.** This bar looks like an '80s hotel lounge—tinted lights, glass brick, and an awesome tropical fish tank. Lots of space to sit and mingle. The '50s-style diner next door is less gay. ⊠ *1501 E. Madison St.,* ☎ *206/726–0565. Crowd: mostly male, over 40, casual.*

**Changes.** The only gay bar north of Lake Union, up in Wallingford and close to the University District, mainly draws people too lazy to drive to Capitol Hill. Fairly small and dark, with pool, pinball, dartboards, and video games, it hasn't much atmosphere, but does lure some outgoing, good-looking folks. ⊠ *2103 N. 45th St.,* ☎ *206/545–8363. Crowd: 75/25 m/f, diverse in age, lesbians from the neighborhood, some students, a nice mix.*

**The Cuff.** Now that the Eagle's gone grunge, this is Seattle's only hangout with a significant leather following—but only on weekends. The large room has a central bar with Tom of Finland posters on the walls and chains dangling about. It's unusually bright. An overflow bar in back opens weekends. Off the side of the main room stretches a narrow patio called the Dog Run. ⊠ *1533 13th Ave. E,* ☎ *206/323–1525. Crowd: male, mostly late-20s and early 30s, low-key, leather but also lots of Levi's, grunge or any look with an edge.*

**Eagle.** Like most Eagles this one began as a leather bar. But perhaps because it's near Capitol Hill's alternative music clubs and several colleges, a young, grungy crowd has begun to hang out here. There's a long dark bar as you enter, a patio out back, an open balcony upstairs overlooking the action, and a smaller cruise bar with pool and pinball. The jukebox plays mostly alternative rock. A lot of guppies from R Place (*see below*) come to the Eagle when they're in the mood for some good-natured sleazing. Friendliest bartenders in town.

✉ *314 E. Pike St.,* ☎ *206/621–7591. Crowd: mostly male, young, a fair racial mix, rough-looking, goatees, a touch of leather, cruisy.*

**The Easy.** Ever since it expanded with a popular restaurant and a big dance floor, this lesbian hangout has attracted a more diverse crowd. The restaurant-bar area is rustic, with rough-hewn wooden floors where you can mingle and cruise, cuddle with a date, or grab a good meal. The other side of the space has bright lights, high ceilings, and the beat of house music most of the time. Of Seattle's two lesbian bars, this one attracts more men and people of color. ✉ *916 E. Pike St.,* ☎ *206/323–8343. Crowd: 80/20 f/m, mostly under 35, varies from lipstick to diesel dykes, a lot of energy.*

**Encore.** You could take your mother to this classy bar and restaurant. Amber lighting and high ceilings are a plus. A good spot to meet up with friends over microbeers or espresso. ✉ *1518 11th Ave. E,* ☎ *206/324–6617. Crowd: 50/50 m/f, all ages, neighborhood types, laid-back, not very cruisy.*

**Kid Mohair.** This upscale lounge has cultivated a big after-work following, with a more energetic crowd arriving later for dancing. Probably more has been spent per square foot on this club than on any West Coast gay bar. One small room downstairs has a dance floor, the other a bar with an extensive beer and wine list. Upstairs there's a cozy balcony with a gas-burning fireplace, plush arm chairs, and even a reproduction antique pay phone—you don't see many of those at a queer bar. Surprisingly, the chichi ambience attracts plenty of cute grungers. Sunday there's a tea dance. Same owners as the nearby Machiavelli restaurant and Bauhaus Books and Coffee. ✉ *1207 Pine St.,* ☎ *206/625–4444. Crowd: 70/30 m/f, mostly mid-20s to late 30s, a few straights, some suits, classy but laid-back.*

**Mr. Paddywack's.** The former Brass Connection now marches to the beat of a different drummer. The major change is the introduction of 25 male dancers, who work the tables and a stage. The club has a strange layout, with a bar up front, a tiny dance floor wedged in back, and a side room with a pool table. ✉ *722 E. Pike St.,* ☎ *206/322–4024. Crowd: 80/20 m/f, mostly 20s and 30s, racially mixed, zero attitude, trampy and fun.*

**Neighbours.** This is Seattle's big gay disco, and though it's neither better nor worse than similar clubs in other towns, it's disappointingly bland in a city that prides itself on alternative culture and music. The decor is industrial, with exposed piping, corrugated metal, and chain-link fences. The music is house. Although there's lots of cruising and standing space surrounding the dance floor, on Fridays and Saturdays you can barely move. The club stays open for dancing after the alcohol is cut off. ⊠ *1509 Broadway Ave.,* ☎ *206/ 324–5358. Crowd: mostly male but some straight females and even fewer dykes; young, white, guppies in disco duds; attitudy, clonish.*

**R Place.** Seattle's cruise palace is a smartly furnished fern bar with three floors. A video bar on the first floor has lots of space for mingling. Seating on the second has a view of downstairs, and there are two pool tables (with almost always a line to play). Upstairs from that is a crowded video bar with loud dance music, another pool table, and lots of room to circulate. For a guppie bar, there's not a lot of attitude. ⊠ *619 E. Pine St.,* ☎ *206/322–8828. Crowd: mostly male, young, professional, button-down, clean-cut, stand-and-model.*

**Re-bar.** For some time this tiny disco has been Seattle's hottest. Every night sees a somewhat queer following—Saturday gets more dykes but Thursday is officially Queer Disco night, with long cruisy lines. The usually postmodern decor changes often. Some determined dancers climb atop the speakers for more elbow room and a chance to vogue. Off the dance floor is a long bar with some seating. Matt Dillon and k. d. lang have been known to pop by (whether on queer or straight nights, no one could confirm). Music ranges from deep house to old new wave to even older disco. Behave yourself on weekends: The bouncer is an enormous drag queen named Isadora. ⊠ *1114 Howell St.,* ☎ *206/233–9873. Crowd: mixed gay/straight; more gay male on Queer Disco nights, but some dykes and groovy straight people; other times young, alternative; Doc Martens and baggy jeans; strong dyke following on Saturday.*

**Thumpers.** This is the kind of bar that settled professional guys head to, often to enjoy dinner at the terrace restaurant or to catch a cabaret act. Since the place has been around for a long time, it has a comfortable feel. With all these successful mature men standing around you can also expect to see a few younger self-starters looking for somebody with deep pockets. ⊠ *1500 E. Madison St.,* ☎ *206/328–3800.*

*Crowd: mostly male, mostly over 40, casual but well dressed with some suits, very clubby.*

**Timberline Tavern.** If you think good country music and line dancing are strictly a southern thing, you're mistaken. This bar is renowned throughout the West Coast. A huge pitched ceiling and rustic post-and-beam construction give it the feel of a western hunting lodge—well, one with a disco ball. The crowd is friendly and energetic, though the women seem to keep to the left and the guys to the right. There's a large dance floor, lots of viewing areas, and a festive back bar. Even if you can't two-step or line-dance, you can come just to watch. The club publishes a handy newsletter with a dance-class schedule and line-dancing instructions: ". . . kick, step, heel, stomp, stamp, stump, bump. . . ." ⊠ *2015 Boren Ave.,* ☎ *206/622–6220. Crowd: 50/50 m/f; all ages; some straights; lots of bolo ties, denim, and cowboy hats.*

**Wildrose.** This mellow lesbian chat spot has an attractive pubby restaurant on one side and a bar with two heavily trafficked pool tables on the other. Big plate-glass windows look onto Pike Street—you can walk by and check out who's inside (too bad more gay bars aren't set up this way). Women often come here before going dancing at the more boisterous Easy across the street. Everyone's welcome if they respect where they are. ⊠ *1021 E. Pike St.,* ☎ *206/324–9210. Crowd: mainly lesbian, mostly 20s and 30s, lots of Doc Martens and baseball caps.*

NEIGHBORHOOD HAUNTS

Seattle has tons of neighborhood joints, and although they're small and draw basically local crowds, they're among the most interesting bars you'll find. Worth noting are **Double Header** (⊠ 407 2nd Ave., ☎ 206/464–9918), which is supposedly the oldest gay bar on the West Coast; **Elite** (⊠ 622 Broadway Ave. E, ☎ 206/324–4470), a real old-timer's bar just down the street from the Broadway Market; **Elite II** (⊠ 1658 E. Olive Way, ☎ 206/322–7334), a fun place for dykes and guys who play pool and darts; **Madison Pub** (⊠ 1315 E. Madison St., ☎ 206/325–6537), good for pool and its selection of imported beers; **Sea Wolf Saloon** (⊠ 1413 14th Ave. E, ☎ 206/323–2158), whose Sunday-night beer bust draws a crowd; **Sonya's** (⊠ 1532 7th Ave., ☎ 206/624–5377), a serious drinking bar that gets going early; and

**Spags** (⊠ 1118 E. Pike St., ☎ 206/322–3232), which calls itself "Seattle's Den for Bears and Trappers."

An honorable mention goes to Jimmy Wu's **Jade Pagoda** (⊠ 606 Broadway Ave. E, ☎ 206/322–5900), an otherwise un-memorable Chinese restaurant with a cozy, womblike bar, substantial gay patronage, a terrific jukebox, and the best Long Island ice teas in town.

### MUSIC CLUBS

Seattle's youthful nightlife scene, much of it centered around Capitol Hill and Belltown, attracts a mix of straights and gays. Below are a few of the bastions of alternative music, fashion, and culture. They tend to draw on open-minded genXers.

The **Comet Tavern** (⊠ 922 E. Pike St., ☎ 206/323–9853), one of the pioneers of grunge music, is almost touristy at this point. Belltown's version of the Comet Tavern, the **Crocodile** (⊠ 2200 2nd Ave., ☎ 206/441–5611), is a major concert venue for cutting-edge bands. The drag cabaret La Cage Seattle is held every Friday at **Downunder** (⊠ 2407 1st Ave., ☎ 206/728–4053), a large dance club. Wednesday is '80s new wave. You can't beat the ambience at **Linda's** (⊠ 707 E. Pine St., ☎ 206/325–1220); filled with Courtney Love and Eddie Vedder wanna-bes, it's a cross between *Twin Peaks* and Pearl Jam. Up-and-coming alternative bands perform here often. **Moe** (⊠ 925 E. Pike St., ☎ 206/324–2406) gets the grunge bunch for coffee, food, and live music; it's queerest on Sunday night. **The Vogue** (⊠ 2018 1st Ave., ☎ 206/443–0673) is a trendy Belltown dance and music club with plenty of bi-curious types racing about.

## Bars in the Burbs and Nearby Cities

The many bars north and south of Seattle are mostly fre-quented by local crowds, all of them open to new blood. North of Seattle in Bellingham, expect good music, plenty of danc-ing, and a mixed gay-male and lesbian crowd at **Rumors** (⊠ 1317 N. State St., ☎ 360/671–1849). Closer to but still north of Seattle, the **Everett Underground** (⊠ 1212 Califor-nia St., Everett, ☎ 206/339–0807) offers more of the same.

The city of Tacoma, 31 miles south of Seattle, has a signifi-cant gay population and a handful of bars. The **24th Street Tavern** (⊠ 2409 Pacific Ave., ☎ 206/572–3748), a butch-

and-bearish pub inside the Grand Central Hotel, draws a mixed gay and straight crowd. The exclusively gay and lesbian **Gold Ball Grill & Spirits** (✉ 2708 6th Ave., ☎ 206/305–9861) has a dance floor. An hour south of Seattle in Washington's capital, Olympia, the enormous disco **Thekla** (✉ 116 E. 5th Ave., down the alley, ☎ 360/352–1855) accommodates between 400 and 500 revelers and is always gay-friendly.

## Action

Favorite Seattle bathhouses include **Basic Plumbing** (✉ 1104 Pike St., ☎ 206/682–8441), which is more of a cruisy sex club than a spa (you don't have to check your clothes); nearby **Club Z** (✉ 1117 Pike St., ☎ 206/622–9958), which is most popular between 10 PM and 2 AM; and **Club Seattle** (✉ 1520 Summit Ave., ☎ 206/329–2334), a traditional "spa." Though it's been around forever, don't overlook **South End Steam Baths** (✉ 115½ 1st Ave. S, ☎ 206/223–9091), a historic landmark.

# SLEEPS

A drawback to visiting Seattle is that you can count on good weather only from about June through September. Since most everyone tries to come at this time, it's very hard to find a room, even out by the airport. In-season rates have risen tremendously over the past five years, but there are still places to stay for less than $100 a night. Just book well ahead. The rest of the year, especially in winter, the town is a bargain. Guest houses, which were unheard of 15 years ago, have boomed recently; you'll find plenty of options on Capitol Hill.

For price ranges, *see* Chart A at the front of this guide.

## Hotels

**$$$$**   🏨 **Alexis Hotel.** Stars and dignitaries often stay at the luxurious Alexis, built in 1901 but decorated with postmodern flair. Many suites have wood-burning fireplaces and Jacuzzis, and all rooms are decorated with a mix of antiques and period pieces. The only drawback to this four-story property is the lack of a view. For a memorable meal, dine in the Painted

Table restaurant (*see* Eats, *above*). ⊠ *1007 1st Ave., 98104,* ☎ *206/624–4844 or 800/426–7033,* FAX *206/621–9009. 109 rooms. Restaurant.*

$$$–
$$$$ ⊡ **Hotel Vintage Park.** A striking 1922 building houses this stylish member of the San Francisco–based Kimpton Group. In keeping with Kimpton's reputation, the hotel is intimate, elegant, and professionally managed—the concierge is one of the most knowledgeable in Seattle. Rooms have cherry-wood furniture and rich, dark fabrics; some have fireplaces. The Italian eatery, Tulio, draws raves all around. ⊠ *1100 5th Ave., 98101,* ☎ *206/624–8000 or 800/624–4433,* FAX *206/ 623–0568. 129 rooms. Restaurant.*

$$$–
$$$$ ⊡ **Sheraton Hotel & Towers.** This 35-story business hotel is at the foot of Pike Street, a hilly but doable walk from most of the gay action. Though it's the site of many conventions, this is one of the most attractive properties in the entire chain. Views from the top-floor health spa are incredible. ⊠ *1400 6th Ave., 98101,* ☎ *206/621–9000 or 800/325–3535,* FAX *206/ 621–8441. 864 rooms. 4 restaurants, pool, health club.*

$$$–
$$$$ ⊡ **Sorrento.** An Italian villa inspired the design of the turn-of-the-century Sorrento. Perched atop First Hill, a short way from Capitol Hill, the hotel has terrific city views. The clubby rooms, more than half of which have separate sitting areas, are filled with antiques, and the staff is well trained and efficient. Celebs such as David Bowie and Debbie Gibson have made it their roost over the years. The Hunt Club restaurant serves excellent cuisine. ⊠ *900 Madison St., 98104,* ☎ *206/ 622–6400 or 800/426–1265,* FAX *206/343–6155. 76 rooms. Restaurant.*

$$$ **The Paramount Hotel.** This WestCoast property is Seattle's newest, which means that its stylish, contemporary rooms have such state-of-the-art amenities as data ports and movie and game systems, along with coffeemakers, hair dryers, and minibars. Executive suites cost only a bit more than double rooms and have whirlpool tubs. ⊠ *724 Pine St., 98101,* ☎ *206/292–9500 or 800/426–0670,* FAX *206/292–8610. 146 rooms. Restaurant, fitness center.*

$$–$$$ ⊡ **Inn at the Market.** Right across the street from Pike Place Market, this relatively young property has the ambience of a French countryside inn—dine downstairs at the hotel's Campagne (*see* Eats, *above*) restaurant if you're not totally convinced. Many of the good-size rooms have unobstructed

views of Elliott Bay. ✉ *86 Pine St., 98101,* ☎ *206/443–3600 or 800/446–4484,* ℻ *206/448–0631. 65 rooms. Restaurant.*

**$$–$$$**   🏨 **WestCoast Plaza Park Suites.** At the foot of Capitol Hill but still above I–5, this all-suites hotel has a terrific location, spacious accommodations (many with fireplace and kitchen), and provides complimentary Continental breakfast. It caters largely to business travelers but is ideal for anyone planning a stay of a few days or more. ✉ *1011 Pike St., 98101,* ☎ *206/682–8282 or 800/426–0670,* ℻ *206/682–5315 194 rooms. Pool.*

**$$**   🏨 **WestCoast Roosevelt Hotel.** Pricier than its nearby cousins, the Camlin and the Vance, this 1930 study in art deco high-rise architecture is more refined and elegant. Rooms run the gamut from budget-priced glorified closets to affordable suites with hot tubs. ✉ *1531 7th Ave., 98101,* ☎ *206/621–1200 or 800/426–0670,* ℻ *206/233–0335. 151 rooms. Exercise room.*

**$–$$**   🏨 **WestCoast Camlin.** With the Roosevelt and the Vance, the Camlin is part of a trio of reasonably priced, restored early 20th-century hotels, all of them downtown and brimming with character. The Camlin is the closest to Capitol Hill. Advantages here include large closets, the quiet atmosphere, and the Cloud Room, a hip and somewhat gay-popular piano bar and lounge on the roof. ✉ *1619 9th Ave., 98101,* ☎ *206/682–0100 or 800/426–0670,* ℻ *206/682–7415. 140 rooms. Restaurant, pool.*

**$–$$**   🏨 **WestCoast Vance.** This renovated old beauty is the least successful of the WestCoast chain's architectural resuscitations. Rooms are small and on the threadbare side, but this is still a good value for downtown Seattle. ✉ *620 Stewart St., 98101,* ☎ *206/441–4200 or 800/426–0670,* ℻ *206/441–8612. 165 rooms. Restaurant.*

**$**   🏨 **University Inn.** Here's a cheap if sterile option up by the University of Washington and Wallingford. Small, modern, and efficiently run, its has a pleasant outdoor pool and a lively location. ✉ *4140 Roosevelt Way NE, 98105,* ☎ *206/632–5055,* ℻ *206/527–4937. 102 rooms. Pool, exercise room.*

## Guest Houses and Small Hotels

**$$–$$$**   🏨 **Capitol Hill Inn.** This 1903 Queen Anne home once served as a bordello. The decor is eclectic yet very homey overall. Two rooms have whirlpool tubs, and one has a tub and a fireplace. Upstairs rooms are brighter but smaller. One drawback: The inn is stuck in an area of Capitol Hill that's overrun with bland mid-rise apartment houses. ⊠ *1713 Belmont Ave., 98122,* ☎ *206/323–1955,* FAX *206/322–3809. 6 rooms, most with private bath. Full breakfast. Mixed gay/straight.*

**$$** 🏠 **Salisbury House.** Mary Wiese and her daughter run this 1904 Craftsman-style property in a quiet residential section of Capitol Hill. Maple floors, coffered ceilings, and leaded-glass windows are among the home's many fine architectural details; rooms are warmed by floral prints, soft duvets, chintz, and other pleasing prints and fabrics. ⊠ *750 16th Ave. E, 98112,* ☎ *206/328–8682. 4 rooms with bath. Full breakfast. Mostly straight.*

**$–$$** 🏠 **Bacon Mansion.** This dramatic Edwardian-style Tudor mansion is just east of the Broadway action. The antiques-filled rooms have lavish architectural details; some have kitchenettes and refrigerators, and one has a two-person soaking tub. A two-story carriage house in back is ideal for groups or two couples traveling together, though there are plans to turn it into two units. ⊠ *959 Broadway Ave. E, 98102,* ☎ *206/329–1864 or 800/240–1864,* FAX *206/860–9025. 7 rooms with phone, most with private bath; 1 carriage house. Continental breakfast. Mixed gay/straight.*

**$–$$** 🏠 **Chambered Nautilus.** A Georgian-style house in the U. District has great views of the Cascade Range and is near to Green Lake Park. There are four sundecks. Now, if only Seattle had sun. ⊠ *5005 22nd Ave. NE, 98105,* ☎ *206/522–2536. 6 rooms, most with private bath. Full breakfast. Mostly straight.*

**$–$$** 🏠 **Gaslight Inn and Howell Street Suites.** The Gaslight is the best of the gay-oriented inns on the Hill, which is saying a lot as there's a number of great ones. The turn-of-the-century house has arts-and-crafts furnishings and oak paneling. There's a large heated pool outside, along with space for sunning. Next door, accommodations at the more contemporary Howell Street Suites have kitchens and large sitting areas. Terrific values, both properties are extremely popular; book well ahead. Trevor Logan and Steve Bennett are delightful hosts. ⊠ *1727 15th Ave. E, 98122,* ☎ *206/325–3654,* FAX *206/324–3135. 14 rooms with TV, most with private bath, some with phone. Pool. Continental breakfast. Mixed gay/straight.*

**$–$$** 🏠 **Hill House.** This 1903 beauty, owned by hosts Ken Hayes and Eric Lagasca, is another of Capitol Hill's perfectly restored Victorians. Rooms are furnished with antiques, lace curtains, and fluffy down comforters. The full breakfast is superb. ⊠ *1113 E. John St., 98102,* ☎ *206/720–7161 or 800/720–7161,* ℻ *206/323–0772. 5 rooms, some with private bath. Full breakfast. Mixed gay/straight.*

$–$$　🏨 **Landes House.** The distinctive Craftsman-style Landes House, which was named after the city's only woman mayor, is right off Volunteer Park. Several rooms have decks with views of Puget Sound and the city skyline. Breakfast here is a real treat. ⊠ *712 11th Ave. E, 98102,* ☎ *206/ 329–8781. 11 rooms. Hot tub. Full breakfast. Mostly mixed gay male/lesbian.*

### Vashon Island

$$　🏨 **Artist's Studio Loft B&B.** Jacqueline Clayton runs this B&B on secluded Vashon Island, an artsy retreat about 45 minutes from downtown Seattle by car and ferry. Her French-influenced country house sits on 5 acres of paths, ponds, wishing wells, arbors, and gardens well traversed by deer, heron, and other wildlife. Two rooms are in a nearby outbuilding, including a full studio with a kitchenette, VCR, four-poster bed, and skylights. A second room in this building is smaller, but no less pleasant. In the main house, there's a large master suite with French doors, lofted ceilings, and skylights. ⊠ *16529 91st Ave. SW, Vashon Island, WA 98070,* ☎ *206/463–2583,* ℻ *206/463–3881. 3 rooms with TV and private bath. Hot tub. Continental breakfast. Mixed gay/straight.*

### Index

$$　🏨 **Wild Lily Ranch B&B.** About an hour northeast of Seattle, these mountain cabins on fir-and-cedar-studded grounds overlooking the Skykomish River offer proximity to hiking, horseback riding, and other outdoor diversions. ⊠ *Box 313, Index 98256,* ☎ *360/793–2103. 3 units with TV and shared bath. Hot tub. Continental breakfast Mixed gay male/lesbian.*

---

# THE LITTLE BLACK BOOK

## At Your Fingertips

**Crisis Clinic Hotline** (☎ 206/461–3222 or 800/244–5767). **Lesbian Health Clinic** (☎ 206/461–4503). **Lesbian Resource Center** (⊠ 1808 E. Bellevue St., No. 204, ☎ 206/322–3953). **Northwest AIDS Foundation** (☎ 206/329–6923). **Seattle Convention and Visitors Bureau** (⊠ 520 Pike St., Suite 1300,

98101, ☏ 206/461–5800). **Seattle Gay Clinic** (☏ 206/461–4540). **Seattle Visitor Center** (⊠ 800 Convention Pl., ☏ 206/461–5840).

## Gay Media

The weekly **Seattle Gay News** (☏ 206/324–4297) is thorough and well written. The pocket-size **Seattle's Alternative Guidebook** (☏ 206/726–9936) has monthly listings of bars and community resources, plus many restaurants.

The **Lesbian Resource Center Community News** (☏ 206/322–3953), a monthly newspaper, carries news features, community resources, and entertainment notes.

**The Stranger** (☏ 206/323–7101) is the more in-your-face of the city's left-leaning entertainment weeklies. More mainstream and comprehensive is **Seattle Weekly** (☏ 206/623–0500). Both have outstanding queer coverage.

### BOOKSTORES

The recently expanded **Beyond the Closet** (⊠ 1501 Belmont Ave., ☏ 206/322–4609), a handsome lesbigay store, has a helpful staff and an unusually good selection of porn and mainstream gay and lesbian periodicals. The **Baily-Coy Bookstore** (⊠ 414 Broadway Ave. E, ☏ 206/323–8842) is a great independent with a significant gay and lesbian following; it's across the street from the Broadway Market. The city's oldest independent bookstore, **Red & Black Books** (⊠ 432 15th Ave. E, ☏ 206/322–7323), also has many gay titles.

**Elliott Bay Book Company** (⊠ 101 S. Main St., ☏ 206/624–6600), in Pioneer Square, one of the best bookstores on the West Coast, has an extensive lesbian and gay section. Another fine mainstream store downtown, **M. Coy Books** (⊠ 117 Pine St., ☏ 206/623–5354), is close to Pike Place Market.

## Working Out

**BQ Workout** (⊠ Broadway Market, 300 Broadway Ave. E, ☏ 206/860–3070) has long been popular with lesbians and gays. The *in* muscle shop, however, is the **World Gym** (⊠ 8th Ave. and Pike St., ☏ 206/583–0640) at the Convention Center, formerly known as Cascade.

# 2 *Out in the* San Juan Islands

*With Port Townsend and Whidbey Island*

**L**ESBIANS AND GAY MEN ARE FAST DISCOVERING the natural beauty, creative spirit, and relative tolerance of the San Juan Islands, a breathtaking archipelago northwest of Seattle. There are only about a dozen queer-frequented B&Bs across this region, which many people visit in conjunction with an excursion to nearby Whidbey Island, the northeastern Olympic Peninsula town of Port Townsend, or the mainland coastal communities of Anacortes and La Conner. But these villages—all within a reasonable drive or drive/ferry ride from Seattle and each other—are packed with diversions, from hiking and beachcombing to gallery hopping and sophisticated dining. If you're single and looking for a social scene, bear in mind that there are no gay bars or restaurants here, and even the queer-friendly accommodations are predominantly straight.

## THE LAY OF THE LAND

The 750-island San Juan archipelago lies north of Seattle and Puget Sound in the Strait of Georgia, east of Vancouver Island and west of the Washington mainland. People inhabit about 60 of the San Juan Islands; regularly scheduled ferries serve only four. San Juan Island, the most developed, is the closest to the Canadian city of Victoria. Orcas Island, the biggest, claims the most spectacular and rugged scenery. The rolling hills and farmland of smaller, sparsely inhabited Lopez Island are reminiscent of Ireland. Franciscan nuns and private landholders control much of Shaw Island.

Washington State ferries depart for the San Juan Islands from the town of Anacortes on Fidalgo Island. One bridge connects Fidalgo Island to the mainland, another to long and narrow Whidbey Island, which snakes in a southerly direction back toward the mainland, only about 20 miles north of Seattle. Port Townsend, on the northeastern tip of the Olympic Peninsula, is a short ferry ride from Whidbey Island. With a little planning and a detailed ferry schedule, you can hop around the region with relative ease.

## San Juan Island

**Friday Harbor** may seem puny, but it's the San Juan Islands' sole incorporated town and only concentrated tourist center. A perfect Friday Harbor afternoon consists of lunch at one of the several informal cafés overlooking the picturesque harbor, and then perhaps two hours of exploring crafts galleries and other shops.

San Juan Island is over-visited but has some gorgeous scenery, particularly on the drive along **West Side Road,** with its views of the Juan de Fuca Strait and the Olympic Peninsula beyond it. This is one of the few roads in the San Juan Islands that runs directly along the shoreline for an extended period.

In the mid-19th century Great Britain and the United States quibbled over the rights to San Juan Island—a grudge that culminated in the Pig War, a petty skirmish that locals speak of today as though the current state of U.S., Canadian, and British relations sprung directly from it. In any case, joint occupation ended in 1872 when the United States wrested possession from Britain. The countries' two respective military installations are preserved today as distinct halves of **San Juan Island National Historical Park** (⊠ Visitor Center, 125 Spring St., Friday Harbor, ☎ 360/378–2240). Follow Cattle Point Road from Friday Harbor to visit pristine 1,200-acre **American Camp** at the southern tip of the island. The camp overlooks the Juan de Fuca Strait and a long sandy beach. There's an always multiplying wild-rabbit population here, and numerous species of migrating birds. The smaller **English Camp,** set on the serene Garrison and Westcott bays at the northwest end of the island—follow Roche Harbor Road from Friday Harbor—has a more manicured feel, with formal gardens and a green lawn that's ideal for picnicking or lying in the sun.

If you're a connoisseur of oysters, you may recognize Westcott Bay, which supplies some of the country's top restaurants with these slippery, slimy alleged aphrodisiacs. You can buy oysters and clams at the **Westcott Bay Sea Farm** (⊠ 4071 Westcott Dr., near Roche Harbor, ☎ 360/378–2489).

The one museum in the islands, the **Whale Museum** (⊠ 62 1st St., Friday Harbor, ☎ 360/378–4710), is a low-key affair. Researchers here track 100 local orcas; photos, skeletons, and an engaging video unravel the mystery of these powerful and graceful animals.

It's not too difficult to glimpse whales from the western shore of San Juan Island. The viewing station beside the lighthouse is just a short walk from the parking area at **Lime Kiln Point State Park** (⊠ 6158 Lighthouse Rd., ☎ 360/378–2044). From here pods of whales frequently drift as close as 100 yards to the coast. Wildflowers brighten the hills above Lighthouse Road in spring.

## Orcas Island

**Orcas Island** balances the size and variety of San Juan Island with the simplicity and quiet of Lopez Island. You'll find decent restaurants and a few cute shops and crafts galleries in the main village of **Eastsound** at the hinge of this island's two crablike prongs, both of which are dotted with B&Bs.

The wooded eastern side of Orcas draws cyclists and hikers. **Mt. Constitution,** the 2,409-foot centerpiece of **Moran State Park,** appears all the higher because it rises from sea level. You can climb a stone observation tower once you've made it to the top (a 6-mile hike from the bottom or a ½-mile one from the parking area near the summit). Many nearby mountains and islands are visible from here. Trails encircle a few bodies of water, including **Cascade** and **Mountain lakes.**

Beyond Moran State Park in the remote village of **Doe Bay,** you'll find groovy, gay-hospitable **Doe Valley Resort** (☎ 360/376–2291). The cabins here are spare (and that's being kind), but the clothing-optional mineral baths will do wonders for aches and pains incurred while hiking, and there's a passable vegetarian restaurant. The property has two beaches and several hiking trails.

Some people stop at Orcas just to browse the wares at **Crow Valley Pottery** (⊠ Horseshoe Hwy., north of the turnoff for West Sound, ☎ 360/376–4260). The two men who run this local fixture have the scoop on nearly everything about the island and its inhabitants. Their shop is inside Orcas Island's oldest structure.

To peruse the island's western half, drive along Deer Harbor Road, just off Horseshoe Highway (a few miles north of the Orcas ferry terminal), through the sleepy and mostly residential bay-side hamlets of **West Sound** and **Deer Harbor,** from which several wildlife-watching cruises depart.

Little **Shaw Island** is just across Harney Channel from the Orcas Ferry Terminal. Franciscan nuns run Shaw's ferry terminal and the tiny neighboring grocery store (which stocks vinegars, jams, and cheeses produced by the sisters at a nearby farm). There are no restaurants, accommodations, or public facilities except for a few campsites (*see* Sleeps, *below*) at **Shaw Island County Park,** an unspoiled tract of beach and greenery at the island's southern tip.

## Lopez Island

Cyclists enjoy the easily sloping back roads of **Lopez Island,** the closest of the developed San Juan Islands to mainland Washington. With its sweeping farms, fruitful orchards, wind-battered clapboard houses, and squiggly inlets and bays, Lopez Island draws comparisons to New England (minus the commercialism) and western Ireland. Lopez has developed a strong following among gays and lesbians, many of whom come back year after year. Quite a few have settled here in the past two decades.

Ferries land at the northern tip of the island. From here it's a two-minute drive to **Odlin County Park** (⊠ Ferry Rd., ☎ 360/468–2496) and its inviting beach. Continue south another 10 minutes, taking a right onto Lopez Road, to legitimately quaint **Lopez Village,** home to most of the island's businesses, including the **Chimera Gallery** (☎ 360/468–3265), a cooperative of local artists, and **Grayling Gallery** (⊠ 3630 Hummel Lake Rd., ☎ 360/468–2779), which showcases the painting, printmaking, and pottery of 10 local artisans.

## Anacortes and La Conner

Most tourists pass west on Highway 20 (from I–5 north) right through **Fidalgo Island,** which is technically one of the San Juans. Fidalgo is connected to the mainland by a short bridge, and it's easy to drive here without ever realizing you're on an island.

There are a few diversions in **Anacortes,** where ferries depart for the other islands. Downtown has a few antiques shops, and nearly 70 buildings are covered with local artist Bill Mitchell's colorful murals depicting a century's worth of Anacortes residents.

The lower half of Fidalgo Island is laced with scenic roads and crowned by Mt. Erie—just a bump compared with the state's higher peaks. La Conner–Whitney Road leads south from Highway 20 to **La Conner,** which once earned its living on fishing (and still hauls in quite a catch) but now is filled with galleries and antiques shops and a few good restaurants. Serious shoppers will find more to do here than on any of the San Juans. Among the area's wealth of preserved Victorian homes, the **Gaches Mansion** (⊠ 2nd and Calhoun Sts., ☎ 360/466–4288) is decorated with period pieces, and the **Skagit County Historical Museum** (⊠ 501 S. 4th St., ☎ 360/466–3365) sits on a hill overlooking town. You can glean a sense of the region's creative tradition by touring the **Museum of Northwest Art** (⊠ 121 S. 1st St., ☎ 360/466–4446).

## Whidbey Island

Because it's within commuting distance of downtown Seattle, **Whidbey Island** receives a steady flow of day-trippers and overnighters. The island is ideal for scenic driving, bicycling, boating, and beachcombing. The charming village of **Langley,** perched atop a cliff in the southeast, has views of Whidbey and the mainland, a handful of good restaurants, and some crafts and antiques shops.

Highway 20 runs the length of the island, passing through several smaller villages and by a few attractions, including **Meerkerk Rhododendron Gardens** (☎ 360/678–1912) in Greenbank; **Ft. Casey State Park** (☎ 360/678–4519), an ideal picnicking and fishing spot just north of Keystone; and **Coupeville,** Washington's second-oldest town. Some of Coupeville's Victorian homes date from the 1830s. The **Island County Historical Museum** (⊠ 908 Alexander St.,

Coupeville, ☎ 360/678–3310) traces Whidbey's fishing, timber, and farming pasts. **Oak Harbor,** the largest community at the island's northern tip, is overdeveloped and not worth a stop.

**Deception Pass State Park** (✉ Hwy. 20, ☎ 360/675–2417) overlooks the deep gorge that cuts between Whidbey and Fidalgo islands. The park has nearly 30 miles of trails, several saltwater beaches, three freshwater lakes, and many campsites. Even if you're just passing through, stop for a peek at the graceful 1930s bridge that spans the gorge (you can see it from the parking lot).

### Port Townsend

The Victorian town of **Port Townsend** at the northeastern tip of the immense Olympic Peninsula (which is larger than some states) beckons visitors with quick and convenient ferry service from the Whidbey Island village of Keystone.

Port Townsend boomed in the late 19th century, when speculators believed it, and not Seattle, would be the Northwest's American railroad terminus. When the city lost out, a severe depression ensued, and only in the later part of this century has the area flourished as a tourist destination and arts colony. Dozens of bed-and-breakfast inns have opened in recent years, but just as many of the elaborate gingerbread painted ladies here are the private homes of artists, writers, and musicians—which may account for Port Townsend's homo-congeniality. Boutiques, galleries, and antiques shops line the historic waterfront and also **Lawrence Street,** a few blocks uptown.

# GETTING AROUND

It's almost impossible to reach or navigate this region without hopping on one of the **Washington State Ferries** (☎ 206/464–6400 or 800/843–3779). You pay only for westbound trips when traveling to the San Juans. Reservation requirements and when you should arrive at the terminal vary depending on the time of day and year. If bringing a car, be in line for the ferry at least an hour before departure during the summer.

Service is at its height from late spring to early fall, but is reasonably frequent during the off-season between the major points. The earliest runs are usually between 5 and 7 in the morning and the latest are between 8 and 10 at night; a few of the shorter, busier routes—such as Mukilteo to Clinton (on Whidbey Island)—operate until midnight.

**To reach Port Townsend:** From Seattle, take the ferry to either Bainbridge Island or Bremerton, and drive north; from the San Juan Islands or points north, take the ferry from Whidbey Island. **To reach the San Juan Islands:** From the United States or mainland British Columbia, take the ferry from Anacortes (about 90 minutes from either Vancouver or Seattle); from Vancouver Island, take the Sidney ferry (which runs once daily, twice in summer) to Friday Harbor. **To reach Whidbey Island:** From Seattle, take the ferry from Mukilteo (below Everett); from points north, drive via Highway 20, which runs between Anacortes and I–5. **To reach Anacortes and La Conner:** From either Seattle or Vancouver, it's a 90-minute drive via I–5; from Vancouver Island, take the ferry from Sidney; from Port Townsend, take the ferry to Whidbey Island and continue north on Highway 20.

If money's not a problem, you'll save time and hassle by flying to the islands. **Harbor Airlines** (☎ 800/359–3220) has service from Seattle's airport to San Juan Island. **Kenmore Air** (800/543–9595) has floatplane service to Lopez, Orcas, and San Juan. **West Isle Air** (☎ 800/874–4434) runs from Anacortes and Bellingham (ideal if you're coming from mainland B.C.) to the same three islands.

Some people will tell you that bringing a car onto the islands is not worth the bother, but this depends on how long you're staying, and how many islands you're visiting. On summer weekends you may have to wait up to three hours at the terminal to board your ferry. If you're planning to stay for a few days or more and are going only to one island, the wait is probably worth it. If you're going for one or two days, or if you're ferrying among three or four islands, consider leaving the car at the long-term lot in Anacortes.

If you arrive in the San Juans without a car, you have several options. Some inns provide pickup service from the terminal and have bikes for your use touring. You can rent a car on San Juan, Orcas, and Lopez islands, but it'll cost at least double what you'd pay on the mainland. You can rent a moped on Orcas or San Juan islands, and bicycles at all three. Rental shops are near the ferry terminals of all three, but bear in mind that both Orcas and San Juan Island are large and hilly; only riders in good shape will find cycling a convenient method of travel. On the other hand, a bicycle allows you to visit the parts of all three islands that are inaccessible to cars.

Lopez, Orcas, and San Juan all have cab service, and San Juan and Orcas have limited bus service. But these options are only practical in a pinch, not for exploring the territory. On Whidbey Island, and in Anacortes, La Conner, and Port Townsend, a car is the way to get around.

# WHEN TO GO

Because nearly everybody hits the San Juan Islands and coastal northwestern Washington in summer, you should consider a visit in spring or fall. Winter is not unromantic, but many businesses shut down. The islands get far less rain than Seattle, which though nearby is affected by an entirely different weather system. Fall and winter bring many gray and rainy days, however. Temperatures are moderate year-round, averaging in the 70s in summer and rarely dipping below freezing in winter (the record-breaking snowfall of '96–'97 was an exception to this rule).

If you come in summer, book your rooms well ahead (never arrive on an island for the night without an advance room reservation), and give yourself plenty of time for catching ferries and getting around.

# EATS

Inspired by the tourist boom and Seattle's emergence as a center of creative regional cuisine, the San Juan Islands have a half dozen serious restaurants, all of them casual and relatively affordable by resort standards. Additionally, Lopez and Orcas have delis and cheap breakfast and lunch spots. Friday Harbor on San Juan Island has at least a dozen of the same.

Port Townsend, La Conner, and Anacortes boast a broader range of dining options. Port Townsend is stronger on funky cafés, whereas La Conner and Anacortes specialize in the unexciting concept of "family dining." On Whidbey Island, Langley has the best dining, with smaller Coupeville a close second. Oak Harbor's dozens of cheap restaurants are mostly of fast-food quality.

## San Juan Island

FRIDAY HARBOR

**$$–$$$** ✕ **Springtree Cafe.** You enter this intimate art-filled restaurant by passing beneath a century-old gnarled elm tree. Inside, feast on steak with scallions, pancetta, and cognac, or shiitake-and-tofu cakes with seared sweet-pea tendrils and coconut-peanut sauce. ⊠ *310 Spring St.,* ☎ *360/378–4848.*

**$** ✕ **Garden Path Cafe.** With a priceless view over Friday Harbor from either the terrace or the small dining room–cum–art gallery inside, the Garden Path is great for a bite before catching the ferry or exploring the shops nearby. Sandwiches, soups, and salads dominate the menu; for breakfast, try the fantastic Belgian waffles. ⊠ *232 A St., Churchill Square,* ☎ *360/378–6255. No credit cards.*

**$** ✕ **Katrina's.** You'll find several good dishes at this cheap downtown Friday Harbor breakfast and lunch spot—basil potato salad, Asian sesame pasta, snapper burgers, and crab sandwiches. A deck is open in spring and summertime. ⊠ *135 2nd St.,* ☎ *360/378–7290. No credit cards.*

NEAR ROCHE HARBOR

**$$$** ✕ **Duck Soup.** Applewood-smoked oysters from nearby Westcott Bay and grilled game hen marinated in rum and lime are a few of the choices at Duck Soup, set in a rustic cabin overlooking a gentle millpond not far from Roche Harbor. The restaurant is renowned for its urbane and eclectic Northwest cooking. ⊠ *3090 Roche Harbor Rd.,* ☎ *360/378–4878.*

## Orcas Island

EASTSOUND

**$$$– $$$$** ✕ **Christina's.** Perched above an Exxon station and set inside a modest old house, Christina's doesn't look like much from the outside. But it's acclaimed among locals for such tempting fare as chèvre grilled in grape leaves with peppers and garlic, or sturgeon grilled on saffron couscous, with tomato, relish, olives, and Swiss chard. Detractors cite the relatively high prices, but few quibble about the quality of the food. ⊠ *N. Beach Rd. and Horseshoe Hwy.,* ☎ *360/376–4904.*

$$–$$$ ╳ **Ship Bay Oyster House.** You won't find any overwrought nouvelle pairings at this steak-and-seafood house in a Victorian farmhouse near Eastsound—just fresh oysters (cooked or raw), mussels, clams, steaks, beef brisket, and bouillabaisse. ⊠ *Horseshoe Hwy., 1 mi east of Eastsound,* ☎ *360/376–5886.*

$$ ╳ **Bilbo's.** It's small and highly popular, so make a reservation before heading to this surprisingly authentic Mexican restaurant in a region not known for such cuisine. Dried garlic and peppers line the walls—they also punch up such tasty fare as mesquite-grilled orange chicken and broiled oysters with salsa verde. Expect plenty of veggie dishes, too. In warm weather you can dine on the patio out front. ⊠ *N. Beach Rd. and Ave. A,* ☎ *360/376–4728.*

OLGA

$ ╳ **Cafe Olga.** Nestled in a wooded hamlet on the southeastern tip of the island, this timber strawberry-packing barn looks fresh out of a fairy tale. The robust affordable fare—Italian sausage and cheese torte, chicken Moroccan pie, eggplant and hummus sandwiches, and blueberry cheesecake—lives up to the fantasy. ⊠ *Olga Rd.,* ☎ *360/376–5098.*

## Lopez Island

LOPEZ VILLAGE

$$–$$$ ╳ **Bay Cafe.** The Bay Cafe's dining room has the ambience of a highly eccentric country store, with a deer head fashioned out of osier, a classic antique guide boat overhead, and Fiesta ware lining the mantel. Though the fare here is similarly off-beat, the kitchen knows exactly how to prepare a flavorful meal. The menu changes often but might feature Dungeness crab polenta with wild mushrooms, followed by grilled black-tiger prawns. Don't miss the trademark crême caramel, which comes with a different sauce each night. One of the region's best restaurants.⊠ *Lopez Village,* ☎ *360/468–3700.*

$ ╳ **Bucky's Grill.** This pubby hangout in the heart of the village is a terrific place to fill up on local gossip and cholesterol-laden ribs, fried fish, burgers, and other casual fare. It's not fancy, but you can't beat it for a warm, satisfying meal. ⊠ *Lopez Village,* ☎ *360 /468–2595.*

$ ╳ **Lopez Island Soda Fountain.** Be sure to stop by this woman-owned old-fashioned luncheonette for great malted-milk

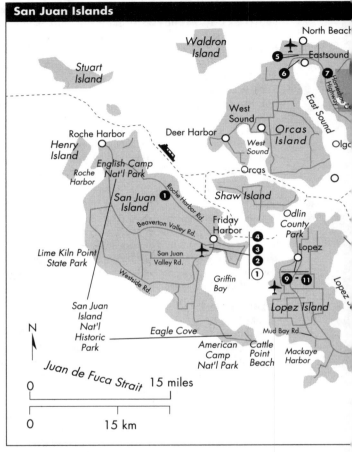

## San Juan Islands

**Eats** ●
Bay Cafe, **9**
Bilbo's, **5**
Bucky's Grill, **11**
Cafe Langley, **16**
Cafe Olga, **8**
Christina's, **6**
Christopher's, **17**

Courtyard
Bistro, **12**
Duck Soup, **1**
Fountain
Cafe, **14**
Garden Path
Cafe, **3**
Katrina's, **2**

Lopez Island
Soda
Fountain, **10**
Palmer's, **13**
Salal Cafe, **15**
Ship Bay Oyster
House, **7**
Springtree
Cafe, **4**

Uptown Oasis
Co., **18**

**Scenes** ○
Front Street Ale
House, **1**

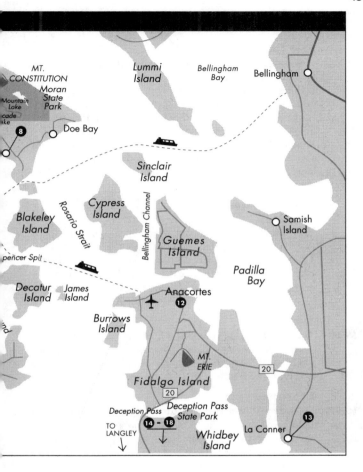

MT.
CONSTITUTION
Moran
State
Park
Mountain
Lake
cade
ke
**8**
Doe Bay

Lummi
Island

Bellingham
Bay

Bellingham

Sinclair
Island

Rosario Strait

Cypress
Island

Blakeley
Island

Bellingham Channel

Guemes
Island

Samish
Island

Padilla
Bay

pencer Spit

Decatur
Island

James
Island

Anacortes
**12**

Burrows
Island

MT.
ERIE

Fidalgo Island
20

Deception Pass
Deception Pass
State Park

TO
LANGLEY
↓

**14** - **18**
↓

La Conner

**13**

Whidbey
Island

20

shakes, floats, and sandwiches. ⊠ *Lopez Village,* ☎ *360/468–3711. No credit cards.*

## Port Townsend

$$–$$$   ✕ **Fountain Cafe.** The talented staff at this Port Townsend favorite has created a thoroughly fashionable, first-rate eatery without making it stuffy or out of character with the spirited town. The menu is heavy on locally grown produce and fish and game. Seafood and pasta dishes are among the best offerings. ⊠ *920 Washington St.,* ☎ *360/385–1364.*

$   ✕ **Salal Cafe.** Eat breakfast or lunch (closing time is 2 PM) amid the hip and creative locals at this employee-owned hangout that's big on sandwiches, omelets, and pastas. Very queer-friendly. ⊠ *634 Water St.,* ☎ *360/385–6532.*

## Whidbey Island

### COUPEVILLE

$$   ✕ **Christopher's.** Christopher Panek, the wunderkind of Pacific Northwest cuisine, presides over this intimate high-ceilinged restaurant that never disappoints. Try oysters broiled with prosciutto and provolone, followed by pork medallions served with a loganberry cream sauce. Getting a table is tough on summer weekends. ⊠ *23 Front St.,* ☎ *360/678–5480.*

### LANGLEY

$$–$$$   ✕ **Cafe Langley.** If you need a lunch or dinner break after boutiquing, this café's Mediterranean-influenced menu makes good use of local seafood. The atmosphere is low-key but elegant. ⊠ *113 1st St.,* ☎ *360/221–3090.*

## Anacortes

$$–$$$   ✕ **Courtyard Bistro.** Few people make a trip to Anacortes solely to dine, but there are a few good casual places and this fine restaurant in the 1889 Majestic Hotel. Though traditional French in spirit, the Bistro serves Continental and Northwest regional dishes, with an especially memorable bouillabaisse in a saffron broth featuring local shellfish. ⊠ *419 Commercial Ave.,* ☎ *360/299–2923.*

### La Conner

**$$–$$$** ✕ **Palmer's.** In an acclaimed eatery one block from the shore, chef Tom Palmer prepares his signature dish: braised lamb shank with roasted garlic and caramelized onions. On the lighter side of the French-influenced menu is the wilted-spinach and smoked-duck salad with a warm sesame dressing. Stained glass surrounds the adjacent authentic re-creation of an English pub, where you can dine on bistro fare and sip microbrewed beers or any of more than 150 wines. ✉ *205 E. Washington St.,* ☎ *360/466–4261.*

## Coffeehouse Culture

Because you're near Seattle finding a good cup of coffee in these small towns is fairly easy. Even tiny Lopez Island has an espresso bar. To find the thriving, slightly queer café culture, check out Port Townsend's brooding-artist coffeehouses and upbeat caffeine stations. The **Uptown Oasis Co.** (✉ 720 Tyler St., ☎ 360/385–2130) is one of the best.

# SCENES

These parts hold only a handful of straight bars, and definitely no gay ones. Northwest Washington is not the place for club-hopping. **Front Street Ale House** (✉ 7 Spring St., ☎ 360/378–2245) in Friday Harbor is one watering hole in the San Juan Islands that's patronized by all types regardless of sexual orientation.

### Action

You and honey (if any).

# SLEEPS

The San Juans hold a zillion B&Bs, but they fill up quickly. From spring through fall, book at least two months in advance. The winter months are nowhere near as hectic, but with many places closed for the season you still need to phone ahead.

Quite a few establishments are owned or run by folks with less than enlightened views toward gays and lesbians. If you can't get a room in one of the B&Bs recommended below, consider staying in one of the overpriced if undercharming motel-style properties on the islands—these are large enough so that you won't have to worry about staff attitudes. Remember that even at the hospitable inns the clientele will be partially if not mostly straight. Camping (*see below*) is another option.

## Guest Houses and Small Hotels

### San Juan Island

FRIDAY HARBOR

**$$**  🖼 **Hillside House.** California transplants Dick and Cathy Robinson completely refitted a suburban-looking contemporary house with chintz, oak furniture, and flagstone walls. Some of the rooms have views of the harbor, others of a two-story aviary in the backyard. Romantics will appreciate the Eagle's Nest suite, which has a cozy double Jacuzzi tub. Hillside House is within walking distance of shops and restaurants. ⊠ *365 Carter Ave., 98250,* ☎ *360/378–4730 or 800/232–4730,* ℻ *360/378–4715. 7 rooms with private bath, 1 with TV. Continental breakfast. Mostly straight.*

**$$**  🖼 **Olympic Lights.** Christian and Lea Andrade run this secluded farmstead near the American Camp National Historical Park. Views from the yellow Victorian farmhouse take in the rustic red barn across the driveway, the Strait of Juan de Fuca, and several mainland mountain ranges. Sunlight streams into window-filled rooms that are decorated in a mostly white color scheme—there's nothing cloying or overly quaint about them. This is one of the nicest inns on the island. ⊠ *4531A Cattle Point Rd., 98250,* ☎ *360/378–3186,* ℻ *360/378–2097. 5 rooms, 1 with private bath. Full breakfast. Mostly straight.*

**$$**  🖼 **Trumpeter Inn.** Guests have full use of this contemporary white house down a dirt road not far from Friday Harbor—the outgoing innkeepers, Don and Bobbie Weisner, live next door. This means you can wander amid the considerable common space, including a music room upstairs and a comfy television area downstairs. Rooms are homey and bright, with fresh flowers, light furnishings, hand-stenciling, and floral prints. ⊠ *420 Trumpeter Way, off San Juan Valley Rd., 98250,* ☎ *360/378–3884 or 800/826–7926,* ℻ *360/378–8235. 5 rooms with private bath. Full breakfast. Mostly straight.*

## Orcas Island

**$$$**  🏨 **Spring Bay.** Former park rangers Carl Burger and Sandy Playa run this handsome new home that's modeled after a turn-of-the-century farmhouse. Every room has a fireplace, a bay view, and a modern bathroom with tile floor; two rooms have a balcony, and one has its own hot tub. Carl and Sandy, who live in a separate house down the hill, lead sea-kayaking tours in the morning, a terrific way to see the surrounding coastline and work off a few pounds. If you're a landlubber, consider hiking amid the inn's 57 acres of wooded hillside. ⊠ *Box 97, Obstruction Pass Rd., Olga 98279,* ☎ *360/376–5531,* ℻ *360/376–2193. 4 rooms with private bath. Hot tub. Full breakfast. Mostly straight.*

**$$–$$$**  🏨 **Windsong.** Built in 1917 as a schoolhouse, later converted into an American Legion hall, and now a B&B, the Windsong has led an interesting life. Innkeepers Kim and Sam have worked hard to turn this into a special retreat, providing such touches as down comforters and rustic but elegant furniture. Rooms, some of which have fireplaces, are named after classical music movements; the Nocturne has tiny stars painted on the ceiling and is filled with southwestern pieces. In general, a spiritual mood permeates the inn. A common hot tub is nestled in a solarium overlooking the rolling lawn behind the house. ⊠ *Box 32, Deer Harbor Rd., Orcas 98280,* ☎ *360/376–2500 or 800/669–3948,* ℻ *360/376–4453. 4 rooms with private bath. Hot tub. Full breakfast. Mostly straight.*

**$$**  🏨 **Kangaroo House.** Rooms in this 1907 Craftsman-style house are small and unfancy, with thin knotty-pine walls and a mix of antiques and older pieces. But the rates are reasonable and the shops and restaurants in Eastsound are a 15-minute walk away. The inn overlooks the airport, which is not necessarily a bad thing—there's little air traffic and the small planes are kind of fun to watch. ⊠ *5 N. Beach Rd., Box 334, Eastsound 98245,* ☎ *360/376–2175. 5 rooms, 2 with private bath. Hot tub. Full breakfast. Mostly straight.*

## Lopez Island

**$$–$$$**  🏨 **Inn at Swifts Bay.** One of the most romantic hideaways in the Northwest has been popular with gays for about a decade. It's run like a first-rate small hotel, but with none of the formality. Guest rooms are exquisitely furnished; the most romantic suite has wine-color walls, skylights, a separate sitting room, and twin showerheads in the bath. There's a common library stocked with books and movies, a hot tub tucked into a garden, and a separate exercise studio with a two-person sauna. Breakfast is a major production, with filling dishes like hazelnut waffles and crab cakes among the memorable offerings. New owners (and former longtime guests) Rob Aney and Mark Adcock took over the inn in the winter of '96–'97. ⊠ *Port Stanley Rd., Rte. 2, Box 3402, Lopez Island 98261,* ☎ *360/468–3636,* 𝔽𝔸𝕏 *360/468–3637. 5 rooms, 3 with private bath, some with TV. Hot tub, exercise room. Full breakfast. Mixed gay/straight.*

**$$**  🏨 **Lopez Farm Cottages.** John Warsen and Ann Warsen rent four cozy cedar cottages on their 30-acre family farm in the heart of the island. Cedar groves, lamb-filled pastures, and orchards surround these contemporary but rustic buildings, each of which have kitchens (minus stoves), fireplaces, and decks—for about the price of a double room at many other inns among the San Juan Islands. Breakfast is delivered in a basket to your room each morning. Three or four more cottages should be completed by the end of 1997. ⊠ *Fisherman Bay Rd., Box 610, 98261,* ☎ *360/468–3555 or 800/440–3556,* 𝔽𝔸𝕏 *360/468–3966. 4 cottages with private bath. Continental breakfast. Mixed gay/straight.*

## Port Townsend

**$$–$$$**  🏨 **James House.** A riot of gables, dormers, and redbrick chimneys adorns Carol McGough's bluff-top, 8,000-square-foot Queen Anne home. Her antiques-laden inn has alluring views of the water and the Olympic and Cascade mountain ranges. Couples or a group of friends traveling together should consider the separate, sunny, relatively contemporary cottage. ⊠ *1238 Washington St., 98368,* ☎ *360/385–1238,* 𝔽𝔸𝕏 *360/379–5551. 13 rooms, some with private bath; 1 cottage. Full breakfast. Mixed gay/straight.*

**$$–$$$**  🏨 **Ravenscroft Inn.** Although it's not one of Port Townsend's elegant old Victorians, this late-1980s mahogany-clapboard inn is a tremendous favorite with gays and lesbians. The innkeepers are professional and outgoing. Rooms contain an attractive mix of antiques and newer pieces. Gardens, laced with a brick walk, surround the house. ⊠ *533 Quincy St., 98368,* ☎ *360/385–2784 or 800/782–2691,* 𝔽𝔸𝕏 *360/385–6724. 8 rooms with private bath. Full breakfast. Mixed gay/straight.*

### Whidbey Island

**$$–$$$** ⌂ **Whidbey Inn.** This Craftsman-style house in the heart of Langley is within walking distance of shops and restaurants. You'll be treated to great views of the water from your room, and also from a deck onto which the three lower rooms open. Owner Dick Francisco owns the eponymous Italian restaurant. ✉ *106 1st St., Box 156, Langley 98260,* ☎ *360/221–7115. 6 rooms with private bath. Full breakfast. Mostly straight.*

Also consider two more Whidbey Island options. Two men rent a one-bedroom waterfront suite—with a color TV, a phone, and a private bath—in downtown Langley (☎ 360/221–2978). Two women in the Bells Beach section of Langley rent a two-bedroom cottage with a kitchenette, a TV and VCR, and dramatic mountain views (☎ 360/730–3766). Both of the accommodations are popular with lesbians, gay men, and straights.

### Anacortes and La Conner

**$$** ⌂ **White Swan.** This 1898 Queen Anne farmhouse and its fertile grounds have been beautifully restored and maintained since Peter Goldfarb purchased it about a decade ago. Each room is named after the color in which it is primarily decorated; one overlooks the tulip gardens in the front yard, another has a cozy turret sitting room. Throughout the house, you can admire Peter's extensive collection of needlepoint samplers. Behind the main house, a cozy cottage with a full kitchen can easily sleep two to four people. Although its address is Mt. Vernon, the White Swan is actually on rural Fir Island, about a 6-mile drive from La Conner. ✉ *1388 Moore Rd., Mt. Vernon 98273,* ☎ *360/445–6805. 3 rooms share 2 baths, 1 cottage. Continental breakfast. Mixed gay/straight.*

## Camping

Campsites in the San Juan Islands area don't have strong gay followings, though Orcas Island's secluded **Doe Island Village Resort** (✉ Star Rte. Box 86, Olga 98279, ☎ 360/376–2291, no reservations) has 50 sites and draws a liberal crowd. **Moran State Park** (✉ Star Rte. Box 22, Eastsound 98245, ☎ 360/376–2326, reservations-by-mail required), has 151 sites. On San Juan Island, try **Lakedale Campground** (✉

2627 Roche Harbor Rd., Friday Harbor 98250, ☎ 360/378–2350 or 800/617–2267, reservations accepted). On Lopez Island, try **Odlin County Park** (✉ Rte. 2, Box 3216, Lopez 98261, ☎ 360/468–2496, reservations for groups and 2 or more nights accepted). Despite having only 12 sites, **South Beach County Park** (✉ Box 86, Lopez Island 98261, no phone, no reservations) at the southern tip of Shaw Island doesn't typically fill up, except on busy summer weekends.

# THE LITTLE BLACK BOOK

## At Your Fingertips
**Anacortes Chamber of Commerce** (✉ 819 Commercial Ave., Suite G, 98221, ☎ 360/293–7911). **Central Whidbey Chamber of Commerce** (✉ 5 S. Main St., Box 152, Coupeville 98239, ☎ 360/678–5434). **La Conner Chamber of Commerce** (✉ 109 S. 1st St., 98257, ☎ 360/466–4778). **Langley Chamber of Commerce** (✉ 124½ 2nd St., 98260, ☎ 360/221–6765). **North Olympic Peninsula Visitor and Convention Bureau** (✉ Box 670, Port Angeles 98362, ☎ 360/452–8552). **San Juan Island Chamber of Commerce** (✉ Box 98, Friday Harbor 98250, ☎ 360/378–5240). **San Juan Islands Tourism Cooperative and Visitors Information Service** (✉ Box 65, Lopez 98261, ☎ 360/468–3663).

## Gay Media
There's not much need for gay newspapers or arts and entertainment weeklies in the San Juan Islands. The free **Book of the San Juan Islands** (☎ 360/378–4191) is a useful guide to local events and establishments. The **San Juanderer** (☎ 360/293–3122), published by the *Anacortes American,* is another fine resource.

# 3 *Out in Vancouver*

**V**ANCOUVER IS NORTH AMERICA'S most international metropolis. Legions of Asians settle here every year, adding to the presence of Brit transplants, Canadians from back East, three different tribes of aboriginal Indians, and a flood of American tourists (Washington State is just 40 miles south). For the past decade nearly 100,000 people have relocated to British Columbia annually, with the majority settling around Greater Vancouver. Is it any surprise that Vancouver has the highest proportion of foreign-born residents of any city in the world?

Temperamentally Vancouver is strongly influenced by the Far East and Great Britain (two, for the most part, orderly regions of the world), and by the Pacific Northwest's natural beauty and moderate climate (how could anybody manage anger in the face of such awe-inspiring surroundings?). Vancouver is thus a little staid, but at the same time an even-keeled, good-humored city where progress is measured more by health and happiness than by socioeconomic status.

Barely a century old, Vancouver looks even newer—like North America's first truly postmodern city. Its contemporary skyline, rife with colorful and angular glass-and-concrete towers, strongly recalls Hong Kong and London's Docklands. Sitting on a peninsula jutting into the rippling Strait of Georgia, sculpted by bays and inlets, Vancouver also reminds one of San Francisco. In both, mountains rise dramatically a short distance from the city center.

Vancouver, Canada's largest city west of Toronto, has the potential to become the country's largest: It is growing faster than any urban center on the continent. Hong Kong entrepreneurs skittish over China's takeover of that island have moved here in record numbers, which has only increased Vancouver's stature as a Pacific Rim business center, and the city trails only New York and Los Angeles in the size of its film industry.

Vancouver's natural beauty is an aesthetic draw, its relative proximity to Asia and access to the Pacific Ocean a strategic draw, and its mild climate and low-key personality a psychological draw. For lesbians and gay men, there are additional lures: highly visible commercial and residential sectors such as Davie Street in the West End and Commercial Drive on the East Side, a compact and friendly nightlife, dozens of social and professional groups, and an accepting citizenry—several of Vancouver's 27 elected officials are gay, as is the suburban member of Parliament, Svend Robinson.

Since August 1969, when Prime Minister Pierre Trudeau's government decriminalized homosexuality, many Canadian cities and provinces have initiated laws and statutes to ensure homosexuals equal rights. In 1996 the federal government passed Bill C-33, which added sexual orientation to the Canadian Human Rights Act, a comprehensive antidiscrimination policy; a few months later the government began extending health benefits to same-sex partners of federal employees. British Columbia has long had a similar law banning discrimination on the basis of sexual orientation—it's even legal for same-sex couples to adopt children here.

Despite the generally enlightened atmosphere, the city's lesbian and gay bookstore, Little Sister's, is embroiled in a ridiculous fight, not against right-wing political or religious groups but against the very federal government that granted gays equal protection.

The battle began in 1987 when Canadian Customs confiscated the shipment of two issues of the *Advocate*. Since that time, Little Sister's has teamed with the British Columbia Civil Liberties Association (BCCLA) to wage an all-out war with customs over its consistent detention and ban of books and periodicals dealing with lesbian, gay, and feminist issues. Until the customs tariff code was amended in 1988, even publications produced expressly for the purposes of safe-sex education were kept from entering the country because many of them contained explicit language and photos.

For 40 days throughout the fall of 1994, the case was heard by the Canadian Supreme Court; Jane Rule, Pierre Berton,

Nino Ricci, Pat Califia, and others testified. In January 1996 the court's ruling came down in two parts, one siding with Little Sisters and the BCCLA, and the other siding with Canadian Customs. The court determined that Canadian Customs had acted improperly and that its system of arbitrarily confiscating shipments of books was flawed. However, the court simultaneously upheld the constitutionality of Canadian Customs' authority to censor materials it deems obscene.

In effect the Canadian Supreme Court implicated Canadian Customs for poor judgment and abuse of its authority—and then reaffirmed its right to continue exercising poor judgment and abusing its authority. Little Sisters and the BCCLA took some solace in the court's mixed ruling, but immediately set in motion an appeal of the second half of the decision. In the meantime, works by such diverse authors as John Preston, Sarah Schulman, Dorothy Allison, James Baldwin, Oscar Wilde, Edmund White, and Susie Bright remain subject to seizure.

That Canadian Customs concerns itself with what should or shouldn't be considered obscene seems preposterous. (In one amusing yet telling episode the titillatingly titled book *Stroke* was held by customs until embarrassed inspectors realized that it was about rowing.) Even more upsetting is the homophobic nature of the customs officials' campaign. Madonna's *Sex*, with its explicit depictions of straight and gay sex, was never detained, it has been argued, because the book was released by a major publisher and sold predominantly through mainstream outlets to a non-gay-specific audience. Vancouver's largest bookstore, Duthie's, claims never to have had a single shipment from the United States detained, let alone permanently confiscated. As a test, Duthie's had an American company ship the store a box of books identical to one that had previously been detained en route to Little Sister's. Not surprisingly, the box passed through untouched by customs. British Columbia–based officials seem obsessed, on the other hand, with any shipment headed directly to a gay bookstore. As a result of this campaign, countless titles, most of them released by U.S. publishers, never make it to the shelves of Canadian bookstores, and others are held for months before being permitted to enter Canada (often damaged as a result of improper handling and storage).

Though the case is at base one of censorship, a larger issue concerns perception that even the most clinical treatment of sexual contact—or the most romantic portrayal of love-making—between like genders is inherently obscene. That people might very well have contracted the AIDS virus because educational material was prevented from entering Canada prior to 1988 is frightening to contemplate. The fact that even today shipments of such materials are mistakenly delayed by overzealous customs officials is even more ironic considering that Vancouver hosted 12,000 delegates to the International Conference on AIDS in the summer of 1996.

Since 1994 it has been legal for a foreigner to obtain citizenship here by establishing domestic partnership with a Canadian citizen—amazingly, an American may move to Canada to enter into a legally sanctioned same-sex relationship, but books with images or language depicting such relationships are routinely confiscated by customs. It's hard to believe that this is happening to a bookstore in one of North America's most tolerant cities, in one of the world's more tolerant countries. But where issues of homosexuality are concerned, the battle between Little Sister's and Canadian Customs proves that the path to a fully tolerant planet is a long and bumpy one.

# THE LAY OF THE LAND

The most heavily populated and most-often-visited section of Vancouver is the compact peninsula that contains the downtown commercial center, the residential West End, and, at the peninsula's northwest tip, Stanley Park. Downtown and the West End more or less fuse without any clear boundary. Thousands of Vancouverites walk to work from their West End apartments, and both halves of the peninsula buzz with pedestrian traffic day and night, making central Vancouver's streets quite safe.

Despite Vancouver's generally lively disposition, the city's many overcast days endow its contemporary towers, sheathed in granite, stucco, brick, concrete, and glass, with a slight gloom instead of the brooding elegance one often finds in older skylines. On sunny days the contemporary cityscape's Mondrianesque colors and shapes spring sharply back to life, the glassed-encased buildings reflecting tree-lined mountains and azure bays.

With Burrard Inlet on the north and east, English Bay on the west, and False Creek on the south, the peninsula effectively separates Burrard Inlet from English Bay and is attached at its southeast to the rest of the city, by way of Gastown and Chinatown. The Burrard, Granville, and Cambie bridges across False Creek connect the peninsula to greener, quieter, and less-settled western and southern Vancouver.

## West End and Yaletown

The **West End,** where the majority of Vancouver's queer population resides, is by no means a gay ghetto. You'll find all types here, from young professionals to senior citizens; in general, it's a middle- to upper-middle-class neighborhood. Most everyone lives in 10- to 25-story apartment buildings, so few West Enders have yards or gardens, and relatively few raise families here. The intense building boom that followed World War II transformed what had been the city's earliest well-to-do suburb into reputedly the most densely populated square mile in North America, containing nearly 45,000 people.

One reason that nobody seems able to prove this startling contention is that no two people can agree on the West End's boundaries. For practical purposes, it's the half of the peninsula west of Thurlow Street. Gays live throughout the neighborhood, but eat, shop, and play primarily along **Denman Street,** which runs north–south, and **Davie Street,** which runs east–west and continues to bustle with activity well beyond Thurlow Street into the Yaletown neighborhood.

Only 10 years ago Davie Street was a tattered avenue of homo and hetero prostitution, but legitimate businesses have opened at a rapid pace and rainbow flags are now commonplace. A couple of favorite gay shopping spots are **Antix** (✉ 1072 Davie St., ☎ 604/682–4161), which stocks the latest in alternative fashion, and **D & R Clothing** (✉ 1112 Davie St., ☎ 604/687–0937) for gay styles.

Denman Street is not nearly as queer and appeals to a slightly older, more settled crowd. There are about six coffeehouses along here and several cheap restaurants serving pizza, deli food, Greek cuisine, and sushi. Club kids might want to check out **Topdrawers** (✉ 1030 Denman St., ☎ 604/684–4861), purveyors of slinky disco and gym gear. At the corner of Denman and Davie there's access to **English Bay Beach,** where the gay presence—and the cruising factor—increases as you walk east toward Burrard Bridge.

Heading east from the West End (away from Denman Street), Davie Street crosses Granville, Seymour, and Richards streets (on which there are several gay and straight clubs), before leading into **Yaletown,** a small neighborhood similar to New York City's SoHo in its popularity among the fine-arts-and-fashion elite. The western half of Yaletown centers on **Hamilton and Mainland streets,** below Smithe Street, where early 20th-century warehouses have been restored and converted into chic restaurants, galleries, and shops—one is even a microbrewery. For stylish gifts, furnishings, and clothing, stop by **Freedom** (✉ 1150 Hamilton St., ☎ 604/688–3163).

Farther east, where Pacific Boulevard runs northward toward the Cambie Bridge, is the more contemporary half of Yaletown. Condos and apartment high-rises have been built on the site of the 1986 Vancouver Expo; filmmakers, designers, and artists are buying up lofts and studios here at an astounding rate.

## Stanley Park

Rugged, beautiful **Stanley Park** is a peninsula of more than 1,000 unspoiled acres of greenery, forests of cedar and Douglas fir, and panoramic maritime vistas. You can drive the circumference, parking at any of the many inexpensive lots to explore 5 miles of beach pathway and several historic park buildings. Near the park's West End entrance **Spokes Bicycle** (✉ Denman and W. Georgia Sts., ☎ 604/681–5581) has bikes for rent. The walk to the park's entrance from the West End takes about 15 minutes. Within the park's borders you'll also find the excellent **Vancouver Public Aquarium** (☎ 604/682–1118) and its Amazon Rain Forest Gallery, which features the reptiles, birds, and vegetation of South America. There's a zoo next to the aquarium.

## Downtown

Vancouver's **downtown** is even more difficult to define than the West End. The most concentrated clump of office buildings is bounded by Thurlow Street to the west, Canada Place Way to the north, Seymour Street to the east, and Smithe Street to the south. East–west-running **Robson Street** is the neighborhood's commercial spine from Denman Street to the **B.C. Place** and new **General Motors Place** sports arenas by False Creek. The seedy blocks south of Robson between Yaletown and the West End are usually considered to be part of downtown.

Just off Robson Street the neoclassical **Vancouver Art Gallery** (✉ 750 Hornby St., ☎ 604/682–4668) displays of the works of many of Canada's best-known artists and houses a considerable cache of paintings by the British Columbia–born Emily Carr. The **Canadian Craft Museum** (✉ 639 Hornby St., ☎ 604/687–8266) presents regional, national, and international exhibits. At either of these museums you can find out about the many crafts and fine-arts galleries around town.

Much of Vancouver's shopping is downtown: There's the **Granville Street Mall,** which is dotted with boutiques between Robson and West Pender streets; the 200-store **Pacific Centre** at the corner of Granville and Georgia streets; and the smaller but no less appealing **Royal Centre** at Georgia and Burrard streets. Robson Street itself contains many high-end shops.

Downtown doesn't overflow with sightseeing options, but possesses several outstanding architectural specimens, ranging from 100-year-old beaux arts and neoclassical beauties to glitzy, postmodern skyscrapers. Most dramatic—and quite controversial—is the brilliant, Colosseum-inspired **Vancouver Public Library** (✉ 350 W. Georgia St., ☎ 604/331–3600), finished with the largest pieces of precast granite cladding in North America. In 1995 the library's designer, Moshe Safdie, created the similarly eye-catching 1,849-seat **Ford Centre for the Performing Arts** (✉ 777 Homer St., ☎ 604/602–0616) across the street.

Consider taking the elevator 553 feet to the **Lookout at the Harbour Center** (✉ 555 W. Hastings St., ☎ 604/689–0421), where you'll be rewarded with 360-degree views of the city and surrounding mountains. Do not dine at the revolving restaurant unless you want to pay a lot for mediocre chow, but you might pop in for a drink.

## Gastown and Chinatown

Just east of downtown at the intersection of Homer and Cordova streets is Vancouver's restored Victorian district, **Gastown.** Near the site of Canada's transcontinental railroad terminus, the neighborhood boomed in the late 19th century as the point from which goods were shipped to Asia. By the 1930s commerce had shifted to other parts of the city, and

Gastown's Victorian buildings were largely left to rot. In the '60s and '70s a major revitalization project was undertaken, and today you can stroll along the neighborhood's cobbled main thoroughfare, **Water Street,** past shops, restaurants, and music clubs patronized largely by straight kids from nearby colleges and the burbs. Both Water and **Cordova** streets are interesting from about Richards Street to Columbia Street. At the corner of Cambie and Water streets, look up at the **Gastown Steam Clock,** the only steam-powered timepiece in the world.

At Columbia, walk south a couple of blocks, where Hastings and Pender streets lead through the third-largest **Chinatown** in North America. This area was also run-down until a recent sprucing up. The **Dr. Sun Yat-Sen Classical Chinese Garden** (⊠ 578 Carrall St., ☎ 604/689–7133), the only formal Chinese garden outside the Republic of China, contains stunning foliage. Many rocks and other traditional materials were used to create the garden, much of them imported from Suzhou, China.

## Commercial Drive

If you continue east on Hastings Street for about a mile beyond Chinatown, you'll reach the foot of **Commercial Drive,** which is the closest Vancouver comes to having an underground arts scene. Originally the city's Little Italy, Commercial Drive is still home to Italian restaurants and shops, most of which don't appear to have been altered since the 1950s. However, you'll also find the city's most concentrated enclave of lesbians, a significant number of grungy genXers, several Jamaican-owned shops and eateries, and a lot of local color—some of it eye-pleasing, some of it not. This stretch, from Broadway down the hill to Hastings, is a rougher, seedier, but rather more characterful neighborhood than Kitsilano (*see below*), which has gone yuppie in recent years. **Beckwoman's** (⊠ 1314 Commercial Dr., ☎ 604/254–8056) here sells clothing, jewelry, drums, and objets d'art. **It's All Fun and Games** (⊠ 1417 Commercial Dr., ☎ 604/253–6727) is a dyke gift emporium. Women head to **Womyn's Ware** (⊠ 896 Commercial Dr., ☎ 604/254–2543) for sex toys, lube, and fetish-wear.

## South and West of Downtown

Strictly speaking, any part of Vancouver's mainland that's west of Main Street is considered the **West Side** (which you don't want to confuse with West Vancouver, a suburb at the northern mouth of Burrard Inlet). The West Side is generally more desirable but also more staid than points east. Although much of this vast residential tract holds little interest to tourists, there are a few worthwhile attractions and one neighborhood ideal for exploring.

From downtown the Granville Bridge passes directly over **Granville Island** (an exit ramp from the bridge or a short ferry ride from the southern tip of Thurlow Street will get you here). After having been transformed during the early 1920s from a modest mudflat into a shipping and processing center for the city's logging and sawmill industries, Granville Island was again reinvented in the mid-'70s, when its then largely defunct businesses were bought up and turned into tourist attractions. Today you'll find a mammoth public market, which houses food stalls, galleries, one-of-a-kind shops, theaters, and artists' studios. Though visitors jam onto Granville Island on summer weekends, the diversions here are worth braving the crowds.

The Burrard Bridge stretches from downtown into **Kitsilano,** Vancouver's counterculture community during the 1960s. The heart of the neighborhood is at the intersection of **Cornwall and Cypress streets,** where you'll find lively cafés and shops. Up the hill and running parallel to Cornwall Street is **West 4th Avenue,** which from Burrard west to MacDonald Street is lined with funky hangouts. This neighborhood probably embodies the city's folksy, holistic, New Age persona more than any other, but it's become less bohemian over the years. Gays and lesbians have a less obvious presence here than in the West End or near Commercial Drive.

Two worthy museums are in Kitsilano, right by the beach in grassy **Vanier Park.** At the **Vancouver Maritime Museum** (⊠ 1905 Ogden Ave., ☎ 604/257–8300) you can explore the Arctic schooner *St. Roch* and examine artifacts that trace Vancouver's rich port history. The **Vancouver Museum** (⊠ 1100 Chestnut St., ☎ 604/736–4431), the country's largest civic museum, is filled with exhibits on the culture and history of the Lower Mainland. Vanier Park is a great place for a picnic or some sunning; the view back across False Creek of the West End and the snowcapped mountains in the distance is priceless.

Continue on West 4th Avenue to reach Vancouver's west-ernmost beaches and parks, all near the **University of British Columbia (UBC).** The esteemed **UBC Museum of Anthropology** (✉ 6393 N.W. Marine Dr., ☎ 604/822–3825) has one of the world's most extensive collections of Northwest Coastal Indian art and artifacts. A bit south of the museum on Marine Drive is secluded and at times cruisy **Wreck Beach.** Not especially sandy or accessible (you must hike down a steep 100-foot trail), it's the city's only more-or-less sanctioned nude beach (at least the illegality of letting it all hang out is overlooked by authorities). The south end of Wreck Beach (to get there follow the signs for trail number 6) is predominantly gay and very popular. Near here also is the 70-acre **UBC Botanical Garden** (✉ 16th Ave. and S.W. Marine Dr., ☎ 604/822–9666) and the serene **Nitobe Memorial Garden,** an authentic Japanese tea and stroll garden.

If you're leaving downtown via the Cambie Bridge, you'll pass by restaurants, shops, and Vancouver's City Hall before finally reaching **Queen Elizabeth Park** at 25th Avenue. The **Bloedel Conservatory** (☎ 604/257–8570) within the park reproduces three climate zones: desert, tropical, and rain forest. Hundreds of exotic birds fly freely inside, and the variety of flora is tremendous. Not too far from here you can continue wandering amid 55 acres of ornamental gardens, placid lakes, sculptures and fountains, and sloping lawns at the **Vandusen Botanical Garden** (✉ Oak St. and 37th Ave., ☎ 604/878–9274).

Running parallel to Cambie Street a few blocks east is **Main Street,** which on its blocks south of 22nd Avenue has many antiques shops and a row of Asian restaurants. The popularity of this neighborhood is rising rapidly, and new businesses are beginning to open up as far south as 30th Avenue. Main Street doesn't exactly roar with personality, but it does possess a little of Commercial Drive's countercultural personality.

## The North Shore

The suburbs east and south of Vancouver offer little in the way of colorful exploring, but the city's **North Shore** (meaning the north shore of Burrard Inlet, encompassing the towns of North Vancouver and West Vancouver) merits at least an afternoon of investigating, particularly if you're an outdoors enthusiast.

From downtown take Highway 99 through Stanley Park to reach Highway 1 (the Trans-Canada Highway). Head east to Capilano Road into **Capilano River Regional Park** (☎ 604/985–7474). Here you have access to the roaring river that runs from the mountains north of Vancouver down to Burrard Inlet; just north of the park, the river has been dammed to form Capilano Lake, a major source of the city's water supply. Just about everybody who visits this park doles out a hefty fee to test their nerves walking across the century-old, 450-foot **Capilano Suspension Bridge,** which swings gently (for the most part) 230 feet above the river below it. The bridge leads into a densely wooded forest dotted with trout ponds and laced with trails. The park is also home to one of the northwest's largest salmon hatcheries. Capilano Road eventually winds its way up to 4,000-foot **Grouse Mountain** (☎ 604/984–0661), a popular ski resort where even nonskiers will enjoy the tram ride to near the mountain's peak.

Back on Highway 1, continue east a few more exits to reach Lynn Valley Road and the similarly beautiful mountain park, **Lynn Canyon** (☎ 604/981–3103), with trails, waterfalls, and views back toward the city. Here, a considerably less crowded (and free) suspension bridge also crosses a steep river canyon. Back where Highway 99 joins Highway 1, you can head west a few miles to reach **Cypress Falls Park** (☎ 604/926–6007), yet another mammoth mountain park ideal for hiking and skiing.

# GETTING AROUND

Flying to Vancouver used to be inconvenient, with relatively few direct flights between the U.S. and Canada. That all changed in February 1995 when the two nations approved the Open Skies agreement, which has inspired two dozen new routes between Vancouver and U.S. cities. A new international terminal opened at Vancouver International Airport in 1996—local queer artists Cheryl Hamilton, Mike Van Der Meer, and Dan Planko created some of the outlandish murals inside. Another recent transportation development has been the introduction of **Amtrak** (☎ 800/872–7245) service between Vancouver and Seattle.

**BC Transit** (☎ 604/521–0400) buses and the **Vancouver Airporter** (☎ 604/244–9888) shuttle link the airport to downtown Vancouver for C$9. A **taxi** ride to downtown costs C$25–C$35 Canadian with tip.

Vancouver is best explored by car, but you can reach the peninsula's many attractions and entertainment options either on foot, by bus, or in a cab (they're easy to hail). This is a relatively convenient city for driving, although parking on the peninsula can be tough; use a lot when possible. Vancouver is probably the largest city in North America whose downtown is not traversed by a single freeway; the worst traffic you're likely to face is approaching the city from the U.S. border or from the Trans-Canada Highway (which cuts through eastern Vancouver before heading north over the Burrard Inlet). Buses are handy and efficient on the peninsula and across the bridges to the south—day passes cost C$4.50. The one-line, rapid-transit SkyTrain is mostly used by commuters.

# WHEN TO GO

Vancouver is a city of festivals. A few of the more popular ones include the **Folk Music Festival** (☎ 604/602–9798; mid-July), the **Chamber Music Festival** (☎ 604/602–0363; late July–early Aug.), the **Fringe Theater Festival** (☎ 604/257–0350; early to mid-Sept.), the **International Film Festival** (☎ 604/685–0260; Oct.), the **International Writers & Readers Festival** (☎ 604/681–6330; Oct.), and the **Women in View Festival** (☎ 604/257–1650; Jan.).

Vancouver celebrates **Stonewall in the Park** (☎ 604/731–1593), a daylong late-June festival in Grandview Park, with entertainers, food vendors, local artisans, and the booths of queer businesses. In early August, Vancouver stages an enormous **gay pride parade and festival** (☎ 604/739–1279), which is centered along Denman Street in the West End.

# EATS

Vancouver is Canada's premier dining city, with an outstanding representation of ethnic foods and its own variation on Pacific Northwest cuisine. This nouvelle-inspired style of cooking emphasizes local produce and such native seafood as salmon, oysters, and crabs, and marries these ingredients with a blend of Asian, Continental, and indigenous, even aboriginal, preparations. The area's climate and soil are excellent for growing grapes, so you'll see some very good British Columbian wines on menus, as well as plenty of Washington and California vintages. As for ethnic cuisines, China, Japan, Korea, Thailand, and India figure prominently in Vancouver's dining landscape, and French, Italian, and Greek cooking are all commonplace. There are also several excellent Jamaican, Latin American, and Mexican eateries.

Some of the most elegant restaurants are downtown along Robson and Alberni streets. Davie and Denman have more of the cheap, gay eats—**Slice of Gourmet Pizza** (⊠ 1152 Denman St., ☎ 604/689–1112) is ideal for a quick bite, but you'll find dozens of other places. Good trendy options can be found in Gastown, in Yaletown, on Commercial Drive (something of a Lesbian Avenger restaurant row), on Cambie Street across the bridge from downtown, on Main Street (between 25th and 30th avenues for East Asian, and around 39th and 40th avenues for Indian), along West 4th Avenue, and in Kitsilano. Bagel fanatics should check out **Siegel's** (⊠ Kitsilano: 1883 Cornwall Ave., ☎ 604/737–8151; ⊠ West End: 1224 Davie St., ☎ 604/685–1121), which is open 24 hours and is famous for its chewy Montréal-style bagels.

Picnickers should check out the **Granville Island Public Market** (☎ 604/666–6477) for fresh vegetables and fruits, rich cheeses, baked breads and sweets, and tasty prepared foods. Or, for baked breads, sandwiches, and muffins, head to **Uprising Bread** (⊠ 1697 Venables St., ☎ 604/254–5635), which is just off Commercial Drive and is usually brimming with cute queerfolk. If you ask, you can get day-old bread at a significant discount.

For price ranges, *see* Chart C at the front of this guide.

## West End, Downtown, and Gastown

$$$– $$$$ ✕ **Alabaster.** The chichi dining hub of Yaletown specializes in Italian-influenced dishes such as monkfish with a scallion-cream sauce, veal steak with polenta, and a risotto with wild mushrooms. A dramatic chandelier hangs high above the dining room, illuminating its ocher tones. In the center, appropriately, stands an alabaster statue of Venus. A popular venue for the city's fashion plates. ⊠ *1168 Hamilton St., ☎ 604/ 687–1758.*

66

**Eats** ●
Alabaster, **21**
Allegro, **20**
Bistro! Bistro!, **27**
CinCin, **7**
Delaney's, **2**
Delilah's, **3**
Doll &
Penny's, **11**

The Edge, **13**
Friends, **15**
Grasshopper, **8**
Hamburger
Mary's, **10**
Homer's, **19**
Indigo, **18**
Le Gavroche, **6**
Liliget, **4**

Limelight, **17**
Lola's, **25**
Luna Cafe, **26**
Luxy Bistro, **9**
Mescalero, **5**
O-Tooz, An
Energie Bar, **16**
The Prow, **22**
Raincity Grill, **1**

Raintree, **24**
Steamworks, **23**
Stepho's, **14**
Taiko, **12**

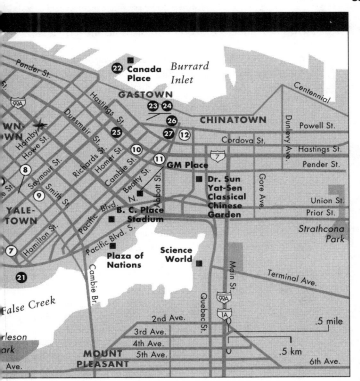

**Scenes** ○
Celebrities, **5**
Denman Station, **1**
Doll &
Penny's, **2**
Heritage House
Hotel, **11**
Hotel
Dufferin, **9**

Mars, **7**
Ms. T's, **10**
Numbers, **4**
The Odyssey, **6**
Our Place
Billiards, **3**
The Royal Hotel
Pub, **8**
Town Pump, **12**

$$$–
$$$$ ✕ **Le Gavroche.** Everybody's favorite classic and contemporary French restaurant is the sort of deeply romantic setting that drives the heart mad—it draws an alarming number of demonstrative lovebirds. A fireplace glows in the dining room of this quaint old stone house on the fringes of the West End; if it's still light out, you'll be treated to views of the mountains north of Vancouver. Oh, almost forgot . . . they serve food, three- and four-course dinners on a menu that changes regularly. Fresh sea bass with white beans, garlic confit, and parsley lemon jus was a recent offering, as was smoked pheasant breast with a delicate truffle sauce. ⊠ *1616 Albernini St.,* ☏ *604/685–3924.*

$$$ ✕ **CinCin.** One of the better power-lunching spots on busy Robson Street will leave you longing for Italy with its fine Mediterranean cooking and Tuscan ambience. Start with the glorious antipasto sampler before having a homemade pasta dish, Dungeness crab cakes with a spicy tomato sauce, or garlic prawns with polenta and lemon. ⊠ *1154 Robson St.,* ☏ *604/688–7338.*

$$$ ✕ **Liliget.** With all the talk about new Pacific Northwest cuisine, you might forget that an aboriginal style of B.C. cooking prevailed in this region long before white settlers arrived. Liliget, which was called Quilicum for many years, preserves this tradition. Toasted seaweed with rice and steamed lemon-herb fern shoots are a couple of the more unusual dishes. Liliget specializes in immense game and seafood platters to share—typical offerings include adler-smoked oysters, and barbecued salmon, buffalo, rabbit, and halibut bits. Native music and art further enhance this unique experience. Very gay-friendly. ⊠ *1724 Davie St.,* ☏ *604/681–7044.*

$$$ ✕ **Lola's.** Stylish and popular with upscale queens, Lola's is a notable purveyor of Pacific Northwest cuisine—grilled squid with a stew of white beans, chorizo, fennel, and lemon; free-range chicken breast stuffed with herb goat cheese, couscous, and preserved lemon; and a great portobello mushroom and falafel burger. Ask to see the innovative "martini menu"—a Molotov cocktail, for instance, has vodka, Irish whiskey, and a dash of Irish Mist. One of the most memorable dining experiences in British Columbia. ⊠ *432 Richards St.,* ☏ *604/684–5652.*

$$–$$$ ✕ **Bistro! Bistro!** One of the best of Gastown's touristy restaurants, this loud, lively bistro has high cedar-beam ceilings, exposed brick, and red and green wicker chairs. Pastas (try

the penne with smoked chicken and mushrooms in garlic and white wine), sandwiches, and seafood grills anchor the menu. *Terrific* crab cakes. ⊠ *162 Water St.,* ☎ *604/682–2162.*

**$$–$$$** ✕ **Delilah's.** Fantastically popular among the gay and straight smart set, Delilah's is *all that* and has been for years. It gets crowded in here, even hectic, as suits mingle over the extensive martini menu and partake of the nouvellish, eclectic, California-meets-Continental menu. Typical are yam soup and pecan-crusted pork loin, but the fare changes often. Such Old World touches as frescoed ceilings and plush furnishings add to the fun. ⊠ *1739 Comox St.,* ☎ *604/687–3424.*

**$$–$$$** ✕ **Indigo.** The ground-floor restaurant of the towering Wall Centre Hotel is popular with executives who work on nearby Robson Street and trendy queers from the West End. The chic dining room has a huge, airy terrace overlooking the street. The food ranges from subtly spicy (crab cakes with sherry and cayenne mayo) to peculiar but satisfying (the seafood chili lasagna). ⊠ *1088 Burrard St.,* ☎ *604/893–7150.*

**$$–$$$** ✕ **Mescalero.** With high ceilings, red-tile floors, Southwest U.S. rugs on the walls, and New Mexico–style tables and chairs, this cavernous, festive restaurant could easily be in Santa Fe. The great pan-American food helps maintain the fantasy with such inventive dishes as grilled pork chops with chipotle, tamarind, and roasted garlic, and chimichangas with Brie, Asiago, and a fruit salsa. Alas, it's devolved into a somewhat obnoxious straight singles scene over the years, but is still tops in the West End for spicy Latin and southwestern fare. Great Chilean wine list. ⊠ *1215 Bidwell St.,* ☎ *604/669–2399.*

**$$–$$$** ✕ **The Prow.** This spot in a glass-walled waterfront dining room beside the Trade and Convention Centre has fine views of Burrard Inlet and the mountains of North Vancouver— it's best to come at lunch or early for dinner, before the sun sets. The food is traditional Continental, with an emphasis on grilled poultry, meats, and seafood (such as baby coho salmon and scallops in a blackberry-tarragon butter). ⊠ *999 Canada Pl.,* ☎ *604/684–1339.*

**$$–$$$** ✕ **Raincity Grill.** Several cuts above the many casual Denman Street eateries, Raincity is one of the hottest places in town. Its contemporary dining room has unusual abstract sconces, polished-wood chairs and paneling, striking floral designs, and a wall of windows looking out toward English Bay. Temptations on the regional menu include oyster stew with spinach and wild-boar bacon, and quail with grilled mesclun and a prosciutto-soya vinaigrette. ⊠ *1193 Denman St.,* ☎ *604/685–7337.*

**$$–$$$**  ✗ **Raintree.** Chef Andrew Skorzewski helped put B.C. regional cuisine on the map, so having a meal here is a lesson in the finer points of inventive cooking and artful presentation. The rustic dining rooms of the Gastown restaurant, with stunning views of Burrard Inlet and the north shore, are fashioned out of native woods and stone, and local art covers the walls, creating a truly authentic Vancouver setting. The menu emphasizes imaginative grills and game dishes, such as smoked Fraser Valley duck breast with a tangy gooseberry compote. Those secure with their figures may wish to partake of the exhaustingly rich sampler dessert platter. ⊠ *375 Water St.,* ☎ *604/688–5570.*

**$$**  ✗ **Allegro.** The owners of the nearby O'Canada House B&B swear by this Mediterranean restaurant, whose homey, festive dining rooms offset its location, a ground floor of a dull downtown high-rise. Ingredients are always fresh, the presentation imaginative, and the prices surprisingly reasonable. Start with tuna carpaccio with pearl onions, capers, dijon mustard, shallots, and lime; move on to grilled New York steak with sun-dried tomatoes, fresh tarragon butter, and seasonal vegetables. Allegro is popular with business lunchers, so you might save a visit for the weekend. ⊠ *888 Nelson St.,* ☎ *604/683–8485.*

**$$**  ✗ **Grasshopper.** The latest slice of fabulosity to strike Davie Street has all the ingredients of a successful café and drinking hole (but then restaurants come and go along this strip, so who knows if it will really last). What it has going for it is an eclectic menu (oven-roasted sea bass, vegetable curry); an adorable patio decked with hanging impatiens and other bright plants and flowers; and a hip cocktail bar where you can sip a martini and look suave without feeling self-conscious (if that's possible). And yes, they do serve grasshoppers—though it's not clear that anybody ever orders them. ⊠ *1262 Davie St.,* ☎ *604/684–4677.*

**$$**  ✗ **Steamworks.** Vancouver has several excellent microbreweries and companion brew pubs, including this loud and social Gastown entry whose ales and lagers are presided over by one of the city's most knowledgeable brew masters. You can savor your stout in any of several rambling dining areas, the most cozy of which is a basement lounge with large-screen

TVs and pool tables. Beer soup, juicy burgers, and crab cakes are among the better options from the affordable menu. Touristy, but with a strong lesbian and gay following. ⊠ *375 Water St.,* ☎ *604/689–2739.*

**$** ✕ **Taiko.** This spare, elegant restaurant inside the Parkhill Hotel has light-wood seating and contemporary lighting. The favorite spot of West Enders for sushi, sashimi, and authentic Japanese cooking, it's one of the best in the city. ⊠ *1160 Davie St.,* ☎ *604/685–1311.*

**$–$$** ✕ **Friends.** This place has lasted in a location that has seen its share of failed culinary ventures. Solid comfort food—potpies, ratatouille, charbroiled chicken fingers—and an unpretentious staff keep folks coming back for more. The classy dining room has dark-blue wicker chairs and neatly framed contemporary art lining its cream-color walls. Many of the friends at Friends are friends of Dorothy's. ⊠ *1221 Thurlow St.,* ☎ *604/685–0995.*

**$–$$** ✕ **Luxy Bistro.** Not as much of a scene as Doll & Penny's (*see below*) but still extremely big with the gay community, this casual storefront restaurant serves humongous portions of pasta. The dining room looks onto Davie Street; the entire wall is open in warm weather. Always a safe bet. ⊠ *1235 Davie St.,* ☎ *604/681–9976.*

**$–$$** ✕ **Stepho's.** The better of two dueling, highly gay-popular Greek tavernas on Davie Street (the other, Taki's, is also good) has a more varied menu, with bounteous Greek salads and many shrimp and lamb dishes. Metaxa bottles and Greek antiques line the walls. ⊠ *1124 Davie St.,* ☎ *604/683–2555.*

**$** ✕ **Doll & Penny's.** Popular for its campy, chaotic decor and cute but air-headed Twinkies (the waiters, not the desserts), Doll & Penny's has fair food and rather distracted service. Still, if you seek the atmosphere of a gay bar in a casual restaurant, you won't be disappointed; it's less about what you eat and more about the crowd you're eating with. ⊠ *1167 Davie St.,* ☎ *604/685–3417.*

**$** ✕ **Hamburger Mary's.** The quality of the food is uneven (and it takes some doing to screw up burgers and fries), but Hamburger Mary's is fun, gay, and closed for only two hours on Fridays and Saturdays. The layout is '50s diner, with glass bricks and vinyl booths. There's more cheese on the jukebox than on the burgers. Great milk shakes, though. ⊠ *1202 Davie St.,* ☎ *604/687–1293.*

$    ✕ **Limelight.** This intimate hole-in-the-wall just up Davie from a few of the gay bars serves healthy, inexpensive Greek and Italian fare, including simple pasta dishes, burgers with various toppings, hot seafood, and several salads. Breakfast is popular here, with smoked salmon Benedict and French toast among the favorites. Very busy on weekends; make reservations. ✉ *1030 Davie St.,* ☎ *604/685–0414.*

$    ✕ **O-Tooz, An Energie Bar.** Best known as a juice bar, this smartly decorated spot also prepares hearty meals. The Cuban black-bean chili is especially good, as are the nonfat frozen yogurt and local baked goods. There are several O-Tooz locations, but the one on Davie draws the city's holistic homos. There are lots of publications on health issues (not to mention the gay papers). ✉ *1068 Davie St.,* ☎ *604/689–0208. No credit cards.*

# Elsewhere in Vancouver

$$$–    ✕ **Tojo's.** As far as most Vancouverites are concerned, mas-
$$$$    ter chef Tojo Hidekazu invented sushi. Fierce with a cleaver yet subtle and artful in his presentations, he tosses scallops and pink cherry blossoms in a light spring salad and creates a sublime golden roll with crab, salmon, and flying-fish roe wrapped in an almost gossamer omelet. Dinner here is no bargain, but Tojo is your man if freshness and quality are of the utmost importance. ✉ *202-777 West Broadway,* ☎ *604/ 872–8050.*

$$–$$$    ✕ **Beetnix.** The name, which conjures up bohemian visions, is a tad misleading. This is a dapper, perhaps even upscale bistro on the hill above Cambie Bridge, near town hall. It has stylish banquette seating and sleek black-and-white tile floors. The Pacific Rim–inspired Continental fare includes mussels with pasta and fennel, and spicy curried-lamb spring rolls. ✉ *2549 Cambie St.,* ☎ *604/874–7133.*

$$–$$$    ✕ **Quattro on Fourth.** One of the more recent additions to Vancouver's burgeoning northern Italian restaurant scene has earned major praise from important critics and ordinary neighborhood folk alike. The spacious dining room has handsomely hand-stenciled walls, and there's a vine-encased wraparound terrace. The menu incorporates pastas and grills in authentic preparations. Enjoy *strozzapreti paesani* (pasta with smoked chicken, black olives, smoked Caciocavallo, and fresh tomato); grilled scallops with wild mushrooms, black

beans, and roasted garlic; or grilled homemade lamb sausage served with cannellini beans. ✉ *2611 W. 4th Ave.,* ☎ *604/ 734–4444.*

**\$–\$\$\$** ✗ **Bridges.** On pleasant days you can dine casually on the deck of this Granville Island favorite, watching the many pleasure craft whisk in and out of False Creek. Indoors you can dine either at a chatty pub serving sandwiches and soups, in the bistro, or in the more formal dining room, where Continental food is featured. ✉ *1696 Duranleau St.,* ☎ *604/687–7351.*

**\$\$** ✗ **Funky Armadillo.** A near-Kitsilano haven of flower children grown up and yuppified, the Armadillo is a splash of colors, energy, and eclectic (vaguely Cajun and southwestern U.S.) fare. The blackened redfish with black-bean mango salsa and wild boar, blue-corn polenta, and the musk ox sausage with grainy dijon and a baguette are some of the flavorful offerings. The walls are covered with music posters (from Louis Armstrong to Jimi Hendrix to Fishbone), and there's live jazz many evenings. ✉ *2741 W. 4th Ave.,* ☎ *604/ 739–8131.*

**\$\$** ✗ **Szechuan Chongqing.** In a city that's been known for outstanding Chinese cooking since before it was incorporated you're rarely going to find a substellar meal. However, unassuming Szechuan Chongqing is tops. The signature house chicken, baked dry on a bed of spinach, is legendary. ✉ *2808 Commercial Dr.,* ☎ *604/254–7434.*

**\$\$** ✗ **Tio Pepe's.** Favorite Yucatan dishes at this sassy little Mexican restaurant include pork served in an achiote marinade and panfried garlic shrimp. Chicken flautas are also a specialty. ✉ *1134 Commercial Dr.,* ☎ *604/254–8999.*

**\$–\$\$** ✗ **Sala Thai.** With a kitchen presided over by a first-generation Thai transplant you can bet that the food here is authentic—and spicy by Canadian standards. Though there are several decent Thai restaurants in the West End, consider a drive across the Cambie Street Bridge to this courtly dining room. ✉ *3364 Cambie St.,* ☎ *604/875–6999.*

**\$–\$\$** ✗ **Sophie's Cosmic Cafe.** Popular with UBC students and anybody with a yen for the absurd, Sophie's looks and feels like an old junk shop, littered as it is with silly toys, old signs, and such oddities as a billiards-table top and balls affixed to the wall. The menu focuses on hearty food—salads, baked salmon, enchiladas, many types of burgers. There's variety in both the eats and the meets. ✉ *2095 W. 4th Ave.,* ☎ *604/ 732–6810.*

**74**

**Eats ●**

Beetnix, **7**
Bridges, **5**
Cafe Deux
Soleil, **14**
Funky
Armadillo, **1**
Harry's, **11**
Juicy Lucy's, **13**
La Grec, **12**
The Naam, **3**
Quattro on
Fourth, **2**
Sala Thai, **9**
Sophie's Cosmic
Cafe, **4**
Szechuan
Chongqing, **15**
Tio Pepe's, **10**
Tomato Fresh
Food, **8**
Tojo's, **6**

**Scenes ○**

Arts Club
Theatre, **2**
Waazubee Cafe, **1**

**Greater Vancouver**

NORTH VANCOUVER

*Burrard Inlet*

TO CAPILANO,
CYPRESS FALLS,
LYNN CANYON

Pipeline Rd.

Vancouver
Public
Aquarium

Stanley Park Drive

*Coal
Harbor*

N

0                    1 mile
0                    1 km

See Downtown Vancouver Map

Ford Centre for
the Performing Arts

GAS-
TOWN

CHINA-
TOWN

Cordova St.

Pender St.

Georgia St.

Robson St.

Haro St.

Thurlow St.

Burrard St.

Howe St.

Hornby St.

Seymour St.

Richards St.

Homer St.

Hamilton St.

Cambie St.

Dunsmuir St.

Hastings St.

Granville St.

Pacific Blvd.

B. C. Place Stadium

Plaza of
Nations

Science
World

Dunlevy Ave.

Powell St.

Hastings St.                    7A

Union St.

Prior St.

Strathcona
Park

Clark

Victoria Dr.

Terminal Ave.

Commercial Dr.

Cambie Br.

Quebec St.

1

Granville
Island

*False Creek*

2nd Ave.

Broadway W.

Hemlock St.

Oak St.

Heather St.

6          7          12th Ave.

16th Ave.

ghnessy
ark
re.

Cambie St.

8
9

28th Ave.

Manitoba St.

Main St.

Fraser St.

Windsor St.

7

Cedar
Cottage
Park

15

Clarke
Park

Knight St.

Victoria Dr.

10
11
12   13
2
14

ng Edward Ave. W.

King Edward Ave. E

1A

99A

andusen
otanical
Garden

33rd Ave.

Queen
Elizabeth
Park

$ ✕ **Cafe Deux Soleil.** Commercial Drive's lesbiqueer house of grunge serves chewy muffins and granola for breakfast, and hefty salads and sandwiches—generally of the vegetarian variety—all day long. At night it's transformed into something of a social hall, with live music and readings. Kid-friendly. ✉ *2096 Commercial Dr.,* ☎ *604/254–1195. No credit cards.*

$ ✕ **Juicy Lucy's.** Dykes come to read the paper on weekend afternoons and sullen grungers sit pensively together at this brightly decorated juice bar and vegetarian café. Needless to say, the people-watching is part of what makes eating here so enjoyable. ✉ *1420 Commercial Dr.,* ☎ *604/254–6101. No credit cards.*

$ ✕ **La Grec.** This might be the best bargain in Vancouver: The Greek food is outstanding, filling, and cheap, with such tasty fare as roast potatoes with rosemary, *tzatziki* (yogurt-cucumber dip) with pita bread, and oysters in a cream sauce. No entrée costs more than $10. Added bonuses are friendly service and an attractive dining room with a red-tile floor, a trompe l'oeil ceiling, and warm, maize-color walls. ✉ *1447 Commercial Dr.,* ☎ *604/253–1253.*

$ ✕ **The Naam.** One of Vancouver's best health-food restaurants is open 24 hours. The tofu burgers are decent and the Thai salads piquant, but the real highlights are the veggie stir-fries and the surprisingly rich desserts. The dining room is cozy and warmly lit; in good weather there's patio seating out back. ✉ *2724 W. 4th Ave.,* ☎ *604/738–7151.*

$ ✕ **Tomato Fresh Food.** There's a retro-diner feel to this sunny sliver of a restaurant just off Cambie Street. A chalkboard menu lists several healthy (mostly Italian-inspired) options, including a fresh and light tomato, basil, and onion salad, and vegetarian chili with corn bread. Beer and wine are served, and you can also try some of the sweet elixirs whipped up at the juice bar. Friendly, mostly gay staff. ✉ *3305 Cambie St.,* ☎ *604/874–6020.*

## Coffeehouse Culture

**Delaney's.** Of Denman Street's several faggy coffee hangouts, Delaney's is everybody's favorite, owing to its handsome skylit sipping room and similarly attractive patrons. The range of desserts and muffins is terrific, but there's no real food. More popular with lesbians than the Edge. ✉ *1105 Denman St.,* ☎ *604/662–3344.*

**The Edge.** With its industrial-gay-bar atmosphere, frantic music, strobe lights, and exposed chrome piping, this is where all the boys (and a few girls) come after the clubs have shut down. Open all night. Great desserts. ⊠ *1148 Davie St.,* ☎ *604/688–3395.*

**Harry's.** Scads of cute dykes shoot pool or pass time at this shabby-chic café with a red linoleum floor, mismatched tables, and a helpful community bulletin board. Near Commercial Drive. ⊠ *1716 Charles St.,* ☎ *604/253–1789.*

**Homer's.** The latest of Vancouver's coffeehouses that feel like bars is actually attached to the Odyssey nightclub—a door from Homer's second-floor balcony leads into the club. You can sip coffee, admire the cute and stylish club-kid bean-grinders behind the counter, or play pool. ⊠ *1249 Howe St.,* ☎ *604/689–2444.*

**Luna Cafe.** One of a handful of popular coffeehouses in Gastown, Luna Cafe has arguably the queerest following. There's an airy seating space, contemporary furnishings, especially good desserts, and the usual array of rich coffees. ⊠ *117 Water St.,* ☎ *604/687–5862.*

# SCENES

Nightlife options in Vancouver are limited for so large a city, mostly because strict licensing regulations make it tough to open new ventures. There has been speculation that the city government will loosen these rules. In the meantime your choices are few, but the clubs you can choose from pack quite a wallop.

Vancouver has always been a down-to-earth city, and though the scene continues to be one of the friendliest in North America the influences of Canada's major party cities (Toronto and Montréal), as well as California's gay strongholds (L.A. and San Francisco), have been felt in recent years. You'll see more guys with rippled bodies clad in the hottest club fashion than you would have a few years back. In general the city's top clubs, though not especially large, have a slick, big-city look about them. A drawback is that most play the same music night after night, and few throw particularly original theme parties.

Vancouver's gay nightlife has as strong an Asian presence as any North American city, though considering the high Asian

population here you'd think it might be even more pronounced; perhaps 10% to 15% of the average bar crowd is
of Asian descent. What's more obvious is how young everybody seems to be. With so many aspiring artists, actors,
filmmakers, and students flocking to Vancouver, the clubs seem
patronized predominantly by twentysomethings.

Despite its visible feminist and lesbian communities, Vancouver is without a full-time women's club. Lesbian events
and parties are thrown constantly, however. The most popular roving get-togethers are sponsored by **Fly Girl** (☎ 604/669–
1753); call for dates and locations. **Little Sister's Bookstore**
(☎ 604/669–1753) usually has information and tickets for
all the women's parties. The **Lotus** (*see* Heritage House Hotel,
*below*) has a lesbian dance party on Friday.

Bars close at midnight on Sundays and at 2 other nights. Friday through Sunday you can almost always count on finding after-hours parties at two or three locations. Ask around.
If you're at one of the discos, keep your eyes peeled near clos-
ing time for someone passing out discount-entry coupons or
flyers for late-night events.

### PRIME SUSPECTS

**Celebrities.** If you're from the States, this club's crowd will
immediately clue you in to British Columbia's drinking age,
which is 19. On Saturday nights it looks like a high school
dance, albeit a fairly racy one. There are bars on both sides
of the main space and a sunken dance floor in the center of
the room, where you'll find several platforms on which to
vogue or pretend you're the most fabulous dancer in North
America. In the back is what appears to have once been a
stage but is now a bar with pool tables. From here you can
head up flights of stairs that lead to a balcony encircling the
dance floor—a good place to stare down at the crowd below
and play "I spy." Celebrities is similar to the Odyssey (*see
below*), but darker in appearance (the walls are black) and
personality. The Wednesday night drag show is a major
event, one of the best in town. ✉ *1022 Davie St.,* ☎ *604/689–
3180. Crowd: young, 80/20 m/f, die-hard club queens and
alternateens; mostly gay but lots of hip, perhaps curious,
straight kids; did we say young?*
**Denman Station.** The only gay nightlife spot on Denman Street
is a large basement video bar. The West End's most convivial
pub, it's a place where gay men and lesbians get together and

dish. It can be surprisingly cruisy, too. Out-of-towners will find this a good place to meet locals. The decor is straight out of the mid-'80s. There's a tiny dance floor, pool tables, and darts. ⊠ *860 Denman St.,* ☎ *604/669–3448. Crowd: 80/20 m/f, mostly 30s and 40s, informal, friendly but a bit cliquey.*

**Heritage House Hotel.** This is an actual hotel, albeit a fairly seedy one. It's best known, however, for its three ground-floor clubs—**Chuck's Pub, Uncle Charlie's,** and the **Lotus**—each with separate entrances. Uncle Charlie's is the least appealing. It's a dated, dull place drawing dowdy regulars. The Lotus is a small, very nice dance club that's only open certain nights. The pillared, low-ceilinged room is especially lively on dyke night (Friday). And then there's Chuck's Pub. No less divey and full of odd characters, it's a colorful tavern with a fire-place, good lighting, a huge neon maple leaf, several big leafy plants, and a few Herb Ritts photos. There's not ex-actly a theme, but it all holds together somehow. Men and women of all ages come here, the bartenders are friendly, and it's not hard to start up a conversation. ⊠ *455 Abbott St.,* ☎ *604/685–7777. Crowd: 70/30 m/f; varies among the 3 bars, but mostly local, working-class, and often eccentric.*

**Hotel Dufferin.** This is a very typical male strip bar, fun if you're in the right mood. No pretenses here. ⊠ *900 Seymour St.,* ☎ *604/683–4251. Crowd: mostly male, over 35, in various stages of undress, unrest, and drunkenness; sleazy, game for a good time.*

**Mars.** This gay-friendly disco has the electricity of an L.A. warehouse disco (though it's smaller). It's the site of many gay parties and special events, especially on Sunday. Sleek and more industrial than the predominantly gay clubs, Mars has a bright dance floor, an amazing sound system, and a small balcony with catwalks. After-hours parties are frequently held following gay events at nearby clubs—the staff usually hands out discount passes to them when Mars is close to shutting down. ⊠ *1320 Richards St.,* ☎ *604/662–7707. Crowd: a mix of straight and gay disco bunnies most of the time; on gay nights it's mostly male and loaded with shirtless gym bun-nies; young crowd.*

**Ms. T's.** Dumpy, downcast, yet strangely enjoyable, the city's drag bar is also the site of the Club Vancouver bathhouse—which is not to suggest that the clientele at one has much to do with that at the other. On Tuesday, people drop in for country-western line-dancing and two-stepping. ⊠ *339 W. Pender St.,* ☎ *604/682–8096. Crowd: mixed m/f, varies according to the night, sometimes quite sparse, other times crowded and campy.*

**Numbers.** It's been around since the old days when Davie Street was one big parade of hustlers, and although the clientele now reflects a broader cross section of the community, the decor doesn't seem to have changed much. There are two levels, plus a small basement lounge called, charmingly, the Kokpit. On the first level there's a little dance floor where dated tunes energize a mostly rhythm-challenged pack of guys. The upstairs is more of a traditional video bar. Porn is shown on several TVs, and there are strippers (who may disrobe entirely in Vancouver) many nights. ⊠ *1042 Davie St.,* ☎ *604/685–4077. Crowd: mostly male, all ages, fun-loving, chickens and chickenhawks, boozy and horny—but in a respectable sort of way.*

**The Odyssey.** Night for night this is Vancouver's hottest gay disco, a midsize club that feels much larger thanks to a mirrored wall on one side. You can enter either by the front entrance on Howe Street or in back through an outdoor patio that's reached from an alley off Davie Street. The patio is a nice place to exchange phone numbers with the cute thing you've met inside. Odyssey's layout is surprisingly interesting for a one-room disco: There's a sunken dance floor on the left side; several steps lead down to it from a viewing area above. You can stand there or on the steps, at the main bar, at a smaller bar in back, or aside the dance floor. The red walls, dim lighting, go-go dancers, and stellar sound system help fuel the libido. ⊠ *1251 Howe St.,* ☎ *604/689–5256. Crowd: 80/20 m/f, very pretty, youngish, stylish, stand-and-model.*

**The Royal Hotel Pub.** A somewhat threadbare hotel, the Royal has an equally run-down but lovable cocktail lounge that's especially crowded on weekdays after work. There's live music some nights—everything from pop to alternative rock to folk. ⊠ *1025 Granville St.,* ☎ *604/685–5335. Crowd: mostly male, older, neighborhood types; more diverse and crowded during concerts.*

OTHER OPTIONS

There are a few alternatives in Vancouver to conventional gay bars. Gastown's **Town Pump** (⊠ 66 Water St., ☎ 604/683–6695) is one of the city's premier live-music venues (this is a top-notch music city; acts ranging from Sarah McLachlan to Loverboy hail from these parts). The queer-fave restaurant **Doll & Penny's** (⊠ 1167 Davie St., ☎ 604/685–3417) has torch singing and live jazz many nights; folks also pile in here to watch *Melrose Place* and the locally filmed *X-Files* on their respective nights.

The black-mascara and pierced-septum set hangs at the **Waazubee Cafe** (⊠ 1622 Commercial Dr., ☎ 604/253–5299), where there's live music. Check *Georgia Straight,* the city's alternative weekly, for other such clubs and events. Vancouver has its own gay pool hall, **Our Place Billiards** (⊠ 1046 Davie St., ☎ 604/682–8368), which is a good place to meet people.

### ONE-NIGHTERS, MOVEABLE FETES

The festive **Arts Club Theatre** (⊠ Back Stage Lounge, next to the Public Market on Granville Island, ☎ 604/687–1644) holds tea dances on the second and fourth Sunday of the month. The dances are great fun, and tend to be stylish affairs (wear your Sunday best).

## Action

Vancouver has a less-bustling bathhouse scene than Toronto and Montréal, but it's still more swinging than in most American cities. Many clubs require that you purchase an annual membership (usually at a nominal cost), for which you'll need to show a government-issued ID, such as a driver's license. **F212° Steam** (⊠ 971 Richards St., ☎ 604/689–9719) is the wildest and busiest of the bunch—it's definitely the hit among out-of-towners and younger guys. Very clean, and the staff is helpful and courteous. **Club Vancouver** (⊠ 339 W. Pender St., ☎ 604/681–5719) isn't as new or well kept, but it's also busy. **Richards Street Service Club** (⊠ 1169 Richards St., ☎ 604/684–6010) has built up a loyal local following during its 30 years as a bathhouse.

# SLEEPS

A stay at the larger mainstream properties on the peninsula will set you back a fair amount, especially in summer: Vancouver receives so much business from the Pacific Rim that its hoteliers can charge relatively high rates. You may be paying for a lot of services and amenities you don't need at these places, which makes one of the smaller European-style hotels a good alternative; the nicest of these are near the West End. There are also many cheap (though dreary) budget accommodations around Gastown and Chinatown, especially on Hastings Street. You might also consider guest houses, several of which are gay-owned or -hospitable (the British Columbia B&B Association informally requires its members to be to queer-friendly). Rates are at their peak from late May through mid-October, but are slashed by as much as 50% in the winter.

For price ranges, *see* Chart C at the front of this guide.

## Hotels

$$$$  🏨 **Sutton Place Hotel.** Despite its immensity the Sutton Place maintains the character of an English manor house—this is Old World hospitality at its best. The clubby Gerard bar is a favorite spot for film celebrities when they're working in town. ✉ *845 Burrard St., V6Z 2K6,* ☎ *604/682–5511; 800/810–6888 in Canada; 800/961–7555 in the U.S.;* 📠 *604/682–5513. 397 rooms. Restaurant, pool, health club.*

$$$$  🏨 **Waterfront Centre.** Non-Canadians may not know as much about the Canadian Pacific hotel chain as they should—these mostly historic hotels are among the most luxurious and professionally staffed in the world. The Waterfront Centre is a postmodern high-rise with terrific views of the adjacent cruise-ship terminal and harbor. Rooms are spacious, with all the deluxe amenities you'd expect. ✉ *900 Canada Place Way, V6C 3L5,* ☎ *604/691–1991 or 800/441–1414,* 📠 *604/691–1838. 489 rooms. Restaurant, pool, health club.*

$$$–  🏨 **Four Seasons.** If you can afford it, camp out at the glam-
$$$$  orous Four Seasons, which rises 28 stories above the snazzy Pacific Centre shopping mall. Airy rooms blend European and Asian art and antiques, the formal Chartwell restaurant is one of the best in the city, and there's an indoor-outdoor pool and an outstanding health spa. This quality here is dramatically high even by luxury-hotel standards. ✉ *791 W. Georgia St., V6C 2T4,* ☎ *604/689–9333; 800/268–6282 in Canada; 800/332–3442 in the U.S.;* 📠 *604/684–4555. 385 rooms. 2 restaurants, pool, health club.*

$$$–  🏨 **Hotel Vancouver.** The Canadian National Railway built
$$$$  the copper-roofed Hotel Vancouver in 1939 (two previous editions also occupied this site), and it's been a beacon of the city's skyline ever since. The hotel retains a dignified air, and

its guest rooms and public areas still recall an earlier era. Renowned California restaurateur Jeremiah Tower helped open the hotel's terrific eatery, 900 West. ⊠ *900 W. Georgia St., V6C 2W6,* ☎ *604/684–3131 or 800/441–1414,* FAX *604/662–1929. 550 rooms. Restaurants, pool, health club.*

**$$–$$$** 🏨 **Coast Plaza at Stanley Park.** Though they're filled with perfunctory chain-hotel furniture, many of the rooms at this 35-story property have outstanding views of the water and mountains, and all have balconies. The Coast Plaza, which often hosts gay events, is in the heart of the West End, a short walk from Stanley Park and English Bay. ⊠ *1733 Comox St., V6P 1P6,* ☎ *604/688–7711; 800/663–1144 in Canada;* FAX *604/688–5934. 267 rooms. Restaurant, exercise room.*

**$$–$$$** 🏨 **Parkhill Hotel.** A stone's throw from several of Davie Street's gay bars and restaurants, this bright new high-rise hotel is less harried and convention-oriented than those downtown. ⊠ *1160 Davie St., V6E 1N1,* ☎ *604/685–1311 or 800/663–1525,* FAX *604/681–0208. 192 rooms. Restaurant, pool, health club.*

**$$** 🏨 **Landis Hotel.** Gays and lesbians frequently choose the Landis, which sits directly behind the Odyssey nightclub. Another of the city's standard high-rises, the Landis is better kept and more efficiently run than many of its more expensive competitors. ⊠ *1234 Hornby St., V6Z 1W2,* ☎ *604/688–1234 or 800/426–0670,* FAX *604/689–1762. 251 rooms. Restaurant, pool, exercise room.*

**$** 🏨 **Buchan Hotel.** Quaint, restored, and smoke-free, this West End property on a tree-lined residential block near Denman Street is a quick walk from Robson Street shopping. Rooms are modestly furnished and many share a bath, but a good number look out at Stanley Park. The management is extremely gay-friendly. ⊠ *1906 Haro St., V6G 1H7,* ☎ *604/685–5354 or 800/668–6654,* FAX *604/685–5367. 60 rooms.*

**$** 🏨 **Sylvia Hotel.** At the immensely popular Sylvia you'll sleep as close to the beach at English Bay as you can without actually waking up with sand in your hair. The eight-story ivy-covered structure has clean rooms with furniture that's so dated it's almost charming. A great value. ⊠ *1154 Gilford St., V6G 2P6,* ☎ *604/681–9321. 119 rooms. Restaurant.*

# Guest Houses and Small Hotels

**$$$**   🏨 **O'Canada House.** Jim Britten and Mike Browne opened this luxurious B&B in 1996. The house was built in 1897; Ewing Buchan composed the national anthem while residing here. The innkeepers have done an incredible restoration job, filling each room with fine antiques as well as every modern convenience you'd want, from VCRs to spacious tile baths. The penthouse has eaved ceilings and skylights—it's great for celebrating romantic occasions. ✉ *1114 Barclay St., V6E 1H1,* ☎ *604/688–0555,* 🖷 *604/488–0556. 4 rooms with phone, TV, and bath. Full breakfast. Mixed gay/straight.*

**$$–$$$**   🏨 **West End Guest House.** This gay-owned pink Victorian is close to downtown and West End attractions. Cozy rooms have sumptuous furnishings and soft, fluffy beds; amenities include VCRs and hair dryers. Charming host Evan Penner, who serves up a filling breakfast, will gladly help you plan your itinerary. A new basement room was added in 1996; although dark, it's large, and ideal for longer stays. ✉ *1362 Haro St., V6E 1G2,* ☎ *604/681–2889,* 🖷 *604/688–8812. 8 rooms with phone, TV, and private bath. Full breakfast. Mixed gay/straight.*

**$–$$**   🏨 **Albion House.** A 10-minute drive from the West End and downtown, this low-key 1906 guest house in a residential neighborhood near Queen Elizabeth Park is perfect for those seeking quiet. The cute, sunny rooms have a mix of antiques and reproductions; one has a balcony overlooking the street. In back there's a deck with an outdoor hot tub. ✉ *592 W. 19th Ave., V5Z 1W6,* ☎ *604/873–2287,* 🖷 *604/879–5682. 4 rooms, some with shared bath. Hot tub. Full breakfast. Mostly mixed gay male/lesbian.*

**$–$$**   🏨 **Colibri B&B.** More contemporary-looking than others in the West End, this stucco house is nonetheless clean and simple with warmly appointed rooms at very reasonable rates. It's a good choice if proximity to Davie Street's nightlife is a priority. Very friendly owners know a great deal about the city—low attitude. ✉ *1101 Thurlow St., V6E 1W9,* ☎ *604/689–5100,* 🖷 *604/682–3925. 5 rooms, all with shared bath. Full breakfast in summer, Continental breakfast in winter. Mostly gay male/lesbian.*

**$–$$**   🏨 **Johnson House B&B.** In the quiet Kerrisdale neighborhood of western Vancouver, this two-tone gray 1920s Craftsman cottage sits behind a rock garden brimming with colorful azaleas and rhododendrons. Hosts Rob and Sandy Johnson

# In case you want to see the world.

At American Express, we're here to make your journey a smooth one. So we have over 1,700 travel service locations in over 120 countries ready to help. What else would you expect from the world's largest travel agency?

do more ®

AMERICAN
EXPRESS

http://www.americanexpress.com/travel

Travel

# In case you want to be welcomed there.

We're here to see that you're always welcomed at establishments everywhere. That's why millions of people carry the
American Express® Card – for peace of mind, confidence,
and security, around the world or just
around the corner.

do more ®

# In case you're running low.

We're here to help with more than 118,000 Express Cash locations around the world. In order to enroll, just call American Express before you start your vacation.

do more

# And just in case.

We're here with American Express® Travelers Cheques
and Cheques *for Two.*® They're the safest way to carry
money on your vacation and the surest way to get a
refund, practically anywhere, anytime.
Another way we help you...

do more

AMERICAN
EXPRESS

**Travelers
Cheques**

have filled their house with unusual collectibles, ranging from antique gramophones and phonographs to barbershop poles. Rooms are filled with antiques, and several have cathedral ceilings; one suite has views of the mountains north of the city. ⊠ *2278 W. 34th Ave., V6M 1G6,* ☎ *604/266–4175. 4 rooms, 3 with private bath. Full breakfast. Mixed gay/straight.*

**$–$$** 🛏 **Nelson House.** The handsome and historic Nelson House is the best of the gay accommodations in the West End, large and rambling, with spacious corner rooms and a suite with a fireplace, a Jacuzzi, and a sundeck. The decor in each room carries a regional theme, from Old World Vienna to Santa Fe. The staff is helpful and quite friendly. ⊠ *977 Broughton St., V6G 2A4,* ☎ *604/684–9793. 5 rooms, some with TV, 1 with private bath. Full breakfast. Mixed gay male/lesbian.*

**$–$$** 🛏 **Penny Farthing.** This striking 1912 Craftsman-style home in Kitsilano has a turquoise exterior with raspberry and white trim, and stained-glass windows and pillar-mantled fireplaces. Friendly innkeeper Lyn Hainstock runs her house with the help of four cats, one of which has earned local acclaim for her ability to play the piano. Rooms are furnished romantically with lace curtains and brass beds or oak four-posters. ⊠ *2855 W. 6th Ave., V6K 1X2,* ☎ *604/739–9002,* 🖷 *604/739–9004. 4 rooms, 3 with private bath. Full breakfast. Mixed gay/straight.*

**$** 🛏 **Columbia Cottage.** This Tudor-style 1920s bungalow is a fine choice across the bridges from downtown. Rooms are small but cheerfully furnished, and the breakfasts are among the tastiest in town. ⊠ *205 W. 14th Ave., V5Y 1X2,* ☎ *604/ 874–5327,* 🖷 *604/879–4547. 4 rooms with private bath and TV. Continental breakfast. Mixed gay/straight.*

## Outside Vancouver

**$–$$** 🛏 **Rural Roots B&B.** It's an hour's drive from Vancouver and 10 minutes from the U.S. border, but this romantic contemporary farmstead is still an ideal base for exploring the city yet escaping its bustle—it's also a good deal less expensive than comparable accommodations in town. The renovated 5,000-square-foot country home is set on 10 pastoral acres of fir and cedar trees. Breakfast is served in a sunny Victorian-inspired conservatory that wraps around one side. The large rooms have separate sitting areas; one has a kitchen. Hosts Jim and Len can tell you all about the area or you can thumb through the handy guidebook they've put together. ⊠ *4939 Ross Rd., Mt. Lehman, BC V4X 1Z3,* ☎ *604/856–2380,* 🖷

*604/857–2380. 4 rooms, most with TV and private bath. Hot tub. Full breakfast. Mostly mixed gay male/lesbian.*

# THE LITTLE BLACK BOOK

## At Your Fingertips

**AIDS Vancouver Help Line** (☏ 604/681–2122). **Everywoman's Health Centre** (☏ 604/322–6692). **Gay and Lesbian Centre of Vancouver** (✉ 1170 Bute St., ☏ 604/684–6869). **Vancouver Lesbian Connection** (✉ 876 Commercial Dr., ☏ 604/254–8458). **Vancouver Status of Women Switchboard** (☏ 604/684–6869). **Vancouver Tourist Info Centre** (✉ 200 Burrard St., ☏ 604/683–2000). *Xtra West* **community hot line** (☏ 604/688–9378).

## Gay Media

*Xtra West* (☏ 604/684–9696) is the community's biweekly, a substantial newspaper that does an excellent job balancing news with entertainment and gay-male with lesbian coverage. Unusual because it's one of the only volunteer-published gay magazines in North America. *Angles* (☏ 604/688–0265) newspaper is published monthly out of the offices of the gay and lesbian center and has both entertainment and news pieces. Also produced by volunteers (ranging from queer youth to longtime activists), it does a great job of informing Vancouver's community. *Kinesis* (☏ 604/255–5499), one of the country's leading feminist papers, devotes considerable attention to gay women.

Vancouver's excellent, free arts-and-entertainment weekly, the *Georgia Straight* (☏ 604/730–7000) focuses frequently on lesbian and gay issues and has fine coverage of local music, film, and theater. *Terminal City* (☏ 604/669–6910) is another arts and political weekly, with a left-leaning slant on Vancouver and northern Washington state; it's thin but filled with alternative and fringe-arts listings.

### BOOKSTORES

**Little Sister's Book and Art Emporium** (✉ 1238 Davie St., ☏ 604/669–1753) has been going strong since 1983 as Western Canada's premier lesbigay bookstore. The shop moved around the corner into a new location in 1996, vastly increasing its inventory and browsing space. There's a great selection of lesbian and gay titles, plus some compact discs, porn videos and magazines, and postcards and greeting cards. The excellent feminist and lesbian-oriented bookstore, **Women in Print** (⌧ 3566 W. 4th Ave., ☎ 604/732–4128), is impressive and comprehensive. It's in Kitsilano, a short drive from the West End.

**Duthie Books** (⌧ 919 Robson St., ☎ 604/684–4496) is a wonderful downtown independent store with a strong gay and lesbian section; it has several other branches around greater Vancouver, including one near Kitsilano (⌧ 2239 W. 4th Ave., ☎ 604/732–5344). The **Magazine Store** (⌧ Robson and Denman Sts., ☎ 604/683–6122) carries foreign and domestic mainstream, gay, and porn magazines and periodicals. On the east side, **Magpie Magazine Gallery** (⌧ 1319 Commercial Dr., ☎ 604/253–6666) offers a similarly strong variety of queer and mainstream mags, plus coffee.

## Working Out
**Fitness World** (West End: ⌧ 1214 Howe St., ☎ 604/681–3232; near downtown: ⌧ 555 W. 12th Ave., ☎ 604/876–1009) is very gay-popular and gets more of the stand-and-model types. Both the **YMCA** (⌧ 955 Burrard St., ☎ 604/681–0221) and **YWCA** (⌧ 580 Burrard St., ☎ 604/895–5777) have homo followings, too. If swimming's your thing, the **Vancouver Aquatic Centre** (⌧ 1050 Beach Ave., ☎ 604/665–3424) is very gay and a bit cruisy.

# 4 *Out in Victoria and Salt Spring Island*

**VISITORS TO WESTERN CANADA** frequently inspire a chuckle from locals by announcing their wish to "spend the day" exploring Vancouver Island. In fact, Vancouver Island is as long as the state of Washington is wide, and the roads traversing much of it are winding and rugged. Vancouver Island does appear small in contrast to the rest of British Columbia, but consider that the province as a whole is larger than any U.S. state excluding Alaska.

With that in mind, every visitor to the city of Vancouver should at least consider a brief excursion to the provincial capital, Victoria, which is at the southern tip of Vancouver Island, or to one of the nearby southern Gulf Islands. Day trips to Victoria or popular Gulf Islands such as Salt Spring are feasible, if a bit costly, by floatplane, and there is ferry service from B.C. and Washington.

A combined car and ferry ride of about 75 minutes separates Victoria and Salt Spring Island, two destinations with charms vastly distinct from each other, as well as from the rest of Canada. Dignified, historic, studded with parks, and packed with some of the nation's most important cultural attractions, Victoria nonetheless feels more like a large town than a full-fledged city. People poke fun at it for being considerably more British than any city in Britain itself, but few deny Victoria's high quality of life and smile-inducing climate.

Salt Spring Island, despite its proximity to Victoria and Vancouver and its somewhat intense summer crowds, retains the quiet, snail-paced personality one might have experienced a century ago. The commercial hub, Ganges Village, feels less cluttered and cheesy than Friday Harbor, its San Juan Islands counterpart. Throughout this wooded, hilly island of nearly 10,000 residents you'll find artists' studios, several fine beaches, hiking and biking terrain, many fishing and sea-kayaking opportunities, and virtually none of Victoria's culture. Visitors come primarily to relax, and to appreciate the serenity and remarkable natural beauty.

Lesbians and gays have long had a presence in Victoria and Salt Spring Island, but there are few resources expressly for the community—no lesbigay papers, bookstores, or community centers, for instance. Victoria has a couple of gay clubs, and in both places you'll find a handful of gay-operated guest houses. Victoria has a high population of retirees and a somewhat suburban feel. The wilds of Salt Spring Island have long been a haven of artists, feminists, New Agers, and other rugged individualists. Attitudes throughout southern Vancouver Island are overwhelmingly tolerant and gay-supportive, but meeting members of the local community—at least in significant numbers—may prove challenging.

# THE LAY OF THE LAND

## Downtown Victoria and the Inner Harbour

Britain's first colony on the Pacific Coast of North America was settled in 1849 as a trading outpost. By the end of the century, when Vancouver was still a mere blip on most maps, Victoria had become B.C.'s capital. The city remains an important political center, but tourists definitely butter the bread these days.

Victoria looks like a typical small British city, only with seagulls, North American accents, and better food. There are few more pleasingly odd views than that of Victoria as you approach the Inner Harbour by boat. In the foreground you'll see the masts of hundreds of colorful sailboats. The formal, London-inspired Parliament Buildings and the Royal Empress Hotel edge the harbor, set against a commanding backdrop of snowcapped mountains.

Downtown is laid out for the most part in an easy-to-follow grid, with Government, Douglas, and Blanshard the main north–south commercial streets; Wharf Street also runs north–south alongside the Inner Harbour before joining with Government Street at James Bay. Most of the shops and restaurants are along these streets, between east–west running Belleville and Johnson streets. Bastion Square, just off Wharf Street, has good dining and shopping. You can walk these diverting blocks in an hour or two.

Downtown is half British confection and half unmemorable contemporary office construction—it's compact and user-friendly, with a low skyline. Gas lamps and cobblestone lanes are everywhere, though there's plenty of British-looking modern electric signage, too. **Centennial Square** (⊠ Pandora Ave. and Government St.) north of the Inner Harbour is one of Victoria's oldest neighborhoods, with many historic buildings. You'll find many antiques and design stores along **Herald, Store, and Johnson streets.** Nearby **Chinatown** is small but contains good eateries and specialty shops; the gate to the district is at Fisgard Street.

Dedicated shoppers can test their spending aptitude at **Market Square** (⊠ 560 Johnson St., ☎ 250/386–2441), definitely one of the more stylish malls in the city, strong on crafts, jewelry, and other handmade items. The 45 shops are set inside a row of historic redbrick buildings. Considerably larger, but less charming and with more run-of-the-mill options, is **Eaton Centre** (⊠ Fort and Government Sts., ☎ 250/389–2228).

The south end of the Inner Harbour contains the government buildings, the imposing **Royal Empress Hotel** (⊠ 721 Government St.), and several noteworthy attractions. You can tour the century-old **Parliament Buildings** (⊠ 501 Belleville St., ☎ 250/387–3046) between 2 and 6 daily. All but fanatics about such things should consider missing the **Royal London Wax Museum** (⊠ 470 Belleville St., ☎ 250/388–4461), just across the street.

Few museums in Canada are more fascinating than the **Royal British Columbia Museum** (⊠ 675 Belleville St., ☎ 250/387–3701), whose artifacts and exhibits document life back 12,000 years in what is now Western Canada. Excellent displays survey aboriginal and colonial life. Most people agree it's Victoria's must-see museum. The **Crystal Garden Con-**

**servatory** (✉ 713 Douglas St., ☎ 250/381–1213) around the corner opened in 1925 with a design that closely recalls the magnificent exhibition halls of 19th-century Europe. More than 65 endangered species make their home in this re-created tropical forest that provides great lessons about preservation and conservation. Look beyond the touristy shopping stalls and restaurants surrounding the conservatory—a tremendous facility lies within.

Just south of here off Douglas Street the 185-acre **Beacon Hill Park** is typically filled with joggers, strollers, and sun worshipers soaking up the atmosphere and the flower-filled aroma. Also a few blocks south of Parliament, **Carr House** (✉ 207 Government St., ☎ 250/383–5843 or 250/387–4697) affords a glimpse into the life of British Columbia's most beloved painter, Emily Carr. She grew up in this wood-frame Victorian; attempts have been made to restore the interior to the way it looked during her childhood.

Walk 15 minutes or drive a short way east of downtown along Fort Street to reach one of B.C.'s greatest house-museums, **Craigdarroch Castle** (✉ 1050 Joan Crescent, ☎ 250/592–5323). This grandiose castle was built by early Victoria industrialist Robert Dunsmuir, who died shortly before the building was completed. Head to the top (fifth) floor for outstanding views of the city.

Just west is the **Art Gallery of Greater Victoria** (✉ 1040 Moss St., ☎ 250/384–4101) one of the top art museums in Western Canada. Its Japanese holdings are among the most comprehensive in North America; other focuses are Canadian, American, and European painting and sculpture. The collection is housed in a Victorian mansion, behind which lies a Japanese garden with the only Shinto shrine outside Japan.

## Greater Victoria and Oak Bay

Once you've exhausted Victoria on foot, consider tooling around the city and its environs by car. A favorite excursion is so-called **Marine Drive,** not the name of any one street but a scenic coastal circuit extending from Ogden Point, which is southwest of the Inner Harbour, to Cadboro Bay. From Ogden Point follow the coastal road alongside the southern end of Beacon Hill Park, past the residential neighborhoods around Ross Bay Cemetery, and wind your way through the

Victoria Golf Club, turning back up through stylish Oak Bay by Cattle Point and up to Cadboro Bay. Terrific views of the Juan De Fuca Strait and Washington's Olympic Mountains unfold the entire way. If you have the time, stop into **Ross Bay Cemetery,** a historic graveyard popular with locals for hiking, walking, and—when the time comes—final repose.

Foul Bay Road runs north–south and separates Victoria from its posh sister, **Oak Bay.** This antidevelopment enclave has some of the area's most prominent homes, as well as commanding water views.

There's not much reason to explore the town of Esquimalt, which is west of downtown Victoria, except for the chance to see a peculiar touch of British camp (unintended, one imagines): a full-size replica of **Anne Hathaway's Cottage** (⊠ 429 Lampson St., ☎ 250/388–4353). The attention to detail in re-creating the early home of playwright William Shakespeare's wife (the original structure is in Stratford-upon-Avon) is impressive, but this attraction, visited by busloads of gawkers, appeals mostly to kids.

Queens, royal and otherwise, typically make it a point to traipse through the 50-odd acres of splendid flower beds at the **Butchart Gardens** (⊠ 800 Benvenuto Ave., ☎ 250/652–4422), a half hour northwest of town—take Highway 17A from downtown. The Butchart family made a fortune manufacturing cement; when they finished mining their quarry, they transformed it into this magnificent collection of gardens. June through September is the best time to visit; on summer nights the gardens are lighted. Thousands of fluttering creatures fly amid the nearby **Victoria Butterfly Gardens** (⊠ 1461 Benvenuto Ave., ☎ 250/652–3833).

A number of companies lead tours through nearby old-growth forests, up rugged mountain peaks, and on whale-watching expeditions. Gay-friendly **Nature Adventures** (☎ 250/480–9560 or 800/840–4453) is one of the most reputable operators.

## Sidney

Ferries from B.C., and some from the U.S. mainland, deposit passengers in **Sidney** (or just north of Sidney, at Swartz Bay), an unassuming and largely uninteresting little town on a peninsula north of Victoria. You will find one moderately engaging attraction, the **Sidney Museum** (⊠ Seaport Palace, 2440

Sidney Ave., ☎ 250/656–2140 or 250/656–1322), whose artifacts and exhibits trace local marine history and also focus extensively on the whales so prevalent in the waters surrounding Vancouver Island. Shops and inexpensive restaurants line the town's main drag, **Beacon Avenue,** a block south.

## Salt Spring Island

Salt Spring Island's nonnative settlers were not Brits, but emancipated black Americans who helped turn the area into a successful farming center in the 1850s. The name of the island is derived from the warm, brackish springs located at its northeast end. Known as Chu-An Island when the British Navy first patrolled the Gulf Islands, the island was officially named "Saltspring" in 1906, but most locals maintain that the Canadian government should never have joined the words together.

Salt Spring remained quiet and sparsely populated for many years, but in the middle of this century, British Columbians began discovering it. Hippies and free spirits moved here in the 1960s, and the mentality remains individualistic and left-of-center to this day.

Despite its popularity among Western Canadians, people in the rest of the country and the United States have only recently begun discovering Salt Spring. Although the island thrives on tourism, little effort has been made to attract larger resorts and chain hotels; this has kept the pace of life slow and easy.

**Ganges Village,** close to the geographic center of the island, holds the community together, with shops and services (including several ATM machines, which are comparatively rare on the neighboring islands), not to mention a couple of espresso bars and a few dozen art galleries. Everything in town is set along a cluster of streets, all within easy walking distance. The town's backdrop is a pine-studded mountain ridge, so you never feel far from nature. **Centennial Park** anchors the village of Ganges, overlooking the harbor. It's a good place to watch the diverse parade of locals, from kids throwing a ball around to New Agers practicing yoga.

Your hope of meeting locals or visitors is greatly enhanced by attending the **Saturday Market** held every Saturday morning in Centennial Park throughout the spring and summer. The market is a great place to buy crafts, crystals, and bric-a-brac, or stock up on organic produce and meats. And cruisy as can be.

On Sunday afternoons from May through October, potters, sculptors, glassblowers, woodworkers, weavers, painters, jewelers, and other artisans open their studios (which are generally in their homes) for browsing. You can pick up a detailed tour map from the chamber of commerce (*see* The Little Black Book, *below*).

**Fulford Harbour,** at the southern end of the island, and **Vesuvius,** to the northwest, are the only other villages of any size. You'll find a handful of basic restaurants and other businesses in each. The pace in each is even slower than in Ganges Village, and both are comparatively untouristy.

Salt Spring Island is shaped almost like three oval lobes strung together width-wise. The southwestern lobe, the least developed, is dominated by the peaks of several small mountains (some of which you can hike). To get to **Mt. Maxwell** from Ganges Village, take Fulford–Ganges Road, turn right onto Cranberry Road, then left onto Mt. Maxwell Road. Hikes to the top of more challenging **Mt. Tuam** can take the better part of a day. You can access the mountain from Fulford Harbour by taking Isabella Road south to Mountain Road. Park at the base and walk up (unless you have a four-wheel-drive vehicle). Not far from here, off Beaver Point Road from Fulford Harbour, you'll find hiking trails at the island's largest park, **Ruckle Provincial Park,** which encloses a farm where sheep wander in great number.

Deer and other wildlife are abundant throughout the Gulf Islands—you're sure to see animals while hiking or cycling (and also while driving, so exercise caution). Years of coexistence with humans has rendered animals quite tame, which means you can sometimes come within a few yards of them (this does not mean you should actually make an effort to approach them).

## The Southern Gulf Islands

Like Salt Spring Island, the neighboring Gulf Islands have green, heavily forested slopes, interrupted only by the occasional rocky promontory. The water around them is dark—almost black. The sun shines here far more than it does in mainland B.C., giving these jewels an enchanting climate. The other islands are sleepier, with cottages clinging to their shores and tiny commercial centers.

**Galiano Island,** a 16-mile sliver of wilderness with about 900 year-round residents, is more remote and wooded than Salt Spring, but still fairly popular with visitors, owing to its vast opportunities for sailing, sea kayaking, scuba diving, and hiking. The island has many fine outdoor outfitters and guides, and several parks with maintained trails. If you have time enough for one additional island, try to come here.

Quiet, squat **Mayne Island,** south of Galiano and east of Salt Spring, has rolling hills and not much in the way of activities, accommodations, or shopping. It's easy to drive or bike the whole island in one afternoon; many visitors come to explore tidal pools, unspoiled beaches, and coastal woodland. The hike up **Mt. Parke** doesn't take more than a half hour; the views of Vancouver and Vancouver Island from the peak are incomparable. Mayne was the first island developed by settlers, but growth has been virtually nil since the turn of the last century. Stop by the **Mayne Museum** (⊠ Plumper Pass Lock Up, ☎ 250/539–5286) for a historical overview.

# GETTING AROUND

## Victoria

Most visitors to Victoria arrive by ferry. From Seattle, you can take the **Victoria Line** (☎ 250/480–5555 or 800/668–1167 in Canada, 206/625–1880 or 800/683–7977 in Washington), which docks at Ogden Point, a short drive or bus ride from the Inner Harbour. This line makes one return trip daily. You can also come from Seattle by way of the more expensive **Victoria Clipper** (☎ 250/382–8100 in Canada, 206/448–5000 or 800/888–2535 in Washington), which runs four times daily in summer and once daily the rest of the year; you'll dock right in the Inner Harbour. The summer-only once-daily **Victoria Express** (☎ 250/361–9144 in Canada, 206/452–8088 or 800/633–1589 in Washington) and four-times-daily **Black Ball Transport** (☎ 250/386–2202 in Canada, 206/457–4491 in Washington), both of which run from Port Angeles on the Olympic Peninsula, also dock at the Inner Harbour.

From Anacortes, Washington, and the San Juan Islands, the **Washington State Ferries** (☎ 604/381–1551 or 604/656–1531 in Canada, 206/464–6400 or 800/843–3779 in Washington) dock in Sidney, about a half-hour drive north of Victoria. From Vancouver, drive about 45 minutes to the port towns of either Tsawwassen or Horseshoe Bay, from which the **B.C. Ferries** (☎ 250/386–3431 in Victoria, 604/669–1211 or 604/277–0277 in Vancouver, 250/537–9921 in Salt Spring, and 250/629–3215 on other southern Gulf Islands) make runs to Swartz Bay eight times daily off-season, and every half hour in summer.

You can also take a **Pacific Coach Lines** (☎ 604/662–8074) bus from Vancouver to Victoria; the trip takes three-plus hours, most of which is spent on the ferry from Swartz Bay to Tsawwassen.

**Air British Columbia** (☎ 800/663–3721) and **Canadian Airlines** (☎ 604/382–6111) both have service from Vancouver and Seattle. **Kenmore Air** (☎ 800/543–9595) has service only from Seattle. Victoria's airport is about 25 minutes north of downtown, near Sidney; there's frequent airport bus service, as well as plenty of taxis. It's more costly, but you can also take a floatplane (a plane that takes off from and lands on the water) from Vancouver to Victoria; try either **Helijet Airways** (☎ 604/273–1414) or **Air B.C. Floatplane Service** (☎ 604/688–5515). If you just want to spend the day in Victoria while in the city of Vancouver, this is the best way to make a quick tour.

If you're planning to stay for more than a night or two, you should strongly consider driving. Even though downtown Victoria is walkable, most of the city is spread out, and a car will allow you explore the outlying areas. Also, many guest houses are beyond walking distance from nightlife and restaurants. Parking is reasonably easy to come by, and this is not a place with chaotic traffic patterns.

If you are here without a car, taxis make sense. You can sometimes hail them on the street downtown, but otherwise phone—try **Empress Taxi** (☎ 250/381–2222). **B.C. Transit** (☎ 250/382–6161) is a practical way to get around much of Victoria; you can buy day passes for C$3, which are good for unlimited travel citywide. You'll also notice that quite a few visitors and locals move around on moped or bicycle; try

**Budget** (✉ 727 Courtney St., ☎ 250/953–5333), within a couple of blocks of the Inner Harbour.

Most guided bus tours of Victoria are fairly typical, but **Blue Line Motor Tours** (☎ 250/360–2249) stands out for its amusing guides and colorful descriptions of the city's history.

## Salt Spring Island
**B.C. Ferries** (*see above*) has limited service from Tsawwassen directly to the Gulf Islands and frequent service from Swartz Bay. Ferries from Tsawwassen, which often stop first at Galiano Island, continue on to Long Harbour (just east of Ganges Village) on Salt Spring Island. The boats from Swartz Bay dock at Fulford Harbour, on the southern tip of Salt Spring. There's also ferry service from Salt Spring Island's Vesuvius Bay to Crofton (about 40 miles north of Victoria) on Vancouver Island.

As with Victoria, most visitors find a car helpful. In summer, however, there can be a great wait getting your car onto a ferry (you can reserve a space for your car to the Gulf Islands, but not from the mainland to Sidney). A speedy, scenic, but more expensive option is flying to Salt Spring by floatplane. Floatplanes depart from one block west of Canada Place, off Burrard Street. The typical cost is C$65 per person each way. **Harbour Air** (☎ 604/537–5525 or 800/665–0212) and **Seair** (☎ 800/447–3247) have regularly scheduled service.

Once on the island you can rent a car, moped, or bicycle to get around; for bikes try **Island Spoke Folk** (✉ 115 Lower Ganges Rd., Ganges Village, ☎ 250/537–4664); **Rainbow Rentals** has scooters (✉ 364 Lower Ganges Rd., ☎ 250/537–2877). You can rent a car (actually for less than a scooter) for about C$30 to C$35 a day; try **Brown's Car Rentals** (☎ 250/537–9333) or **Heritage Car & Truck Rentals** (☎ 250/537–4225), which also has scooters.

**Saltspring Taxi** (☎ 250/537–9712) is a 24-hour taxi service. **Saltspring Transit** (☎ 250/537–4737 or 250/537–1846) has bus service between Ganges Village and the outlying ferry terminals, and from north end of the island to the south. Fares of C$3 to C$5 will get you where you need to go.

# WHEN TO GO

Victoria glows with flower blossoms from February through November, and has an outstanding climate year-round. Many festivals take place throughout the summer. This is prime visiting time, when finding a room in the city can be difficult. The deeply patriotic **Canada Day** is celebrated on July 1. The eight-day **Folk Fest** (☎ 250/388–4728) takes place in late July. Several boat races occur between May and August. Salt Spring Island is most popular from late spring through October, but don't discount a winter visit to either Victoria or the Gulf Islands. Many businesses will be shut down, but the weather is still relatively mild.

# EATS

### Victoria

The quality of cuisine in Victoria is quite high. You'll find seafood and ethnic restaurants, and many places specializing in Pacific Northwest cooking. Owing to the city's British traditions, it's easy to find such Anglophilic meals as fish-and-chips, bangers and mash, and meat pies. Trendy eateries have opened around the Inner Harbour in recent years, several of them catering to a queer clientele.

Should anybody recommend that you take "high tea" at the Royal Empress Hotel, consider a more affordable, less stuffy, and in some ways more charming alternative: the **Point Ellice House** (⊠ 2616 Pleasant St., just off Bay St., ☎ 250/380–6506 or 250/387–4697). This grand house, the only remaining residence in a now-industrial area north of downtown, dates from the 1860s. Afternoon tea has been served for many years on the croquet lawn, amid period-style gardens. Call ahead for reservations.

$$–$$$   ✕ **Camille's.** Several top young chefs teamed together to open this study in diverse foods and culinary styles. Local produce and meats are prepared in a healthful manner; daily specials reflect a different ethnic menu, and the regular offerings are eclectic, too. Typical are warm confit of duck with orange slices and seasonal greens, and roast venison with juniper and rosemary demi-glace and wild-mushroom risotto. ⊠ 45 Bastion Sq., ☎ 250/381–3433.

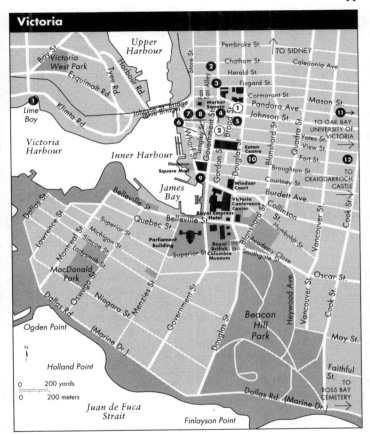

**Eats ●**

Bohematia, **6**
Camille's, **8**
Dilettante's, **10**
Friends of
Dorothy's, **5**
Herald Street
Caffe, **2**
The Java, **4**
Marina, **11**

Milestones, **9**
Pluto's, **12**
Q Cafe, **3**
Reebar, **7**
Spinnakers, **1**

**Scenes ○**

B. J.'s, **1**
Rumors, **2**

**$$–$$$** ✗ **Herald Street Caffe.** Jazz wafts over the din of chatter at this hip, art-filled space in an old redbrick building in the warehouse district just north of downtown. Inventive fish grills change daily, and there are great pastas. Seafood minestrone with a hot-and-sour sauce and cilantro pesto is one of the better starters. Excellent wine list. ⊠ *546 Herald St.,* ☎ *250/381–1441.*

**$$–$$$** ✗ **Marina.** The enormous plate-glass windows at this restaurant on an Oak Bay marina open up to fine views of the water and distant mountains in Washington. Fortunately, the nouvelle-inspired seafood dishes (such as grilled marlin with an orange-sesame vinaigrette) and pastas are much more than an afterthought. There's a well-patronized little sushi bar off to one side. ⊠ *1237 Beach Dr.,* ☎ *250/598–8555.*

**$$–$$$** ✗ **Milestones.** The only Victoria restaurant directly on the Inner Harbour is close to shopping and the two gay clubs. Casual dishes include fish-and-chips, pot stickers, eggplant dip, and pizzas, but there's also a more formal menu with steak, poultry, and seafood. Tourists overrun this place in summer. ⊠ *812 Wharf St.,* ☎ *250/381–2244.*

**$$** ✗ **Dilettante's.** Three extraordinary local chefs, Jennifer Canterbury, Tracey Gilmour, and Naomi Wyse, run this affordable lesbian- and gay-popular café that's ideal for lunch, weekend brunch, and dinner. Sample pistachio-crusted free-range duck or a phyllo crust filled with goat cheese, artichokes, mushrooms, sun-dried tomatoes, Swiss chard, and pine nuts. Five different variations on eggs Benedict are among the lures to Sunday brunch. ⊠ *787 Fort St.,* ☎ *250/381–3327.*

**$$** ✗ **Spinnakers.** Canada's first in-house brew pub opened a few years back in a striking historic building downtown. In addition to oatmeal stout and other rich concoctions, Spinnakers serves up pizzas, sandwiches, and grills. Some say you'll get the best steak in town here. ⊠ *308 Catherine St.,* ☎ *250/386–2739.*

**$–$$** ✗ **Pluto's.** Young, funky guppies and yuppies frequent this colorful, vibrant restaurant that serves mesquite grills, Cajun specialties, juicy burgers, stir-fried veggies, and beef satays. A popular choice before hitting the bars. ⊠ *1150 Cook St.,* ☎ *250/385–4747.*

**$** ✗ **Bohematia.** This recent addition to Victoria's thriving café scene quickly developed a queer following. A cozy nook with muted colors and closely spaced tables, it's an easy place to meet like-minded souls. Whole and organic foods, including a tasty garbanzo-bean salad, are the menu staples, and there's a long list of innovative teas and coffees. Few elixirs take the chill off a damp morning better than spiced blueberry tea with steamed milk and brown sugar. ⊠ *515 Yates St.,* ☎ *250/383–2829.*

$ ✕ **Friends of Dorothy's.** Victoria's only certifiably gay restaurant is run by the owners of B.J.'s (*see* Scenes, *below*) across the street. Drop in for a light lunch—mostly sandwiches, soups, and salads. ⊠ *615 Johnson St.,* ☎ *250/381–2277.*

$ ✕ **ReeBar.** A favorite of gays, artists, and activists, ReeBar is a terrific café with a diverse menu of Asian, Mexican, and healthful regional dishes, plus an extensive beer and wine list. If your energy is sapped from a day of sightseeing, come in for one of the specialty juice combos, including one made of carrots, apples, beets, and ginger. ⊠ *50 Bastion Sq.,* ☎ *250/ 361–9223.*

## Salt Spring Island

For a small island you'll find surprisingly sophisticated cuisine, mostly in Ganges Village, but also in Vesuvius and Fulford Harbour. The gay dollar accounts for a significant chunk of Salt Spring Island's tourist revenues, so expect a warm welcome everywhere. Two tips: For bread, baked goods, organic coffee, and cheerful hellos, check out **Barb's Buns** (⊠ Creekside Marketplace, Ganges Village, ☎ 250/537–4491), which is right beside the **Mobile Organic Market** (☎ 250/537–1784), a good place for picnic supplies. Don't bother dining at **Kanaka** (⊠ Harbour Bldg., Ganges Village, ☎ 250/537–5041)—the food is ordinary at best. But do grab a drink on the deck overlooking the harbor, which often has views of cute navy personnel.

$$$ ✕ **House Piccolo.** A small, unprepossessing house on a side street downtown holds one of the Gulf Islands' most celebrated restaurants. Piccolo serves a blend of regional, Continental, and Scandinavian dishes. Start off with a dollop of Russian caviar, and move on to boneless breast of duck with a mandarin-orange napoleon and green-pepper jus. Local art is framed against the whitewashed walls. The atmosphere here is elegant but still informal. ⊠ *115 Hereford Ave., Ganges Village,* ☎ *250/537–1844.*

$$–$$$ ✕ **Al Fresco.** Fruit-print tablecloths and bright colors enliven Al Fresco's airy dining room, but as the restaurant's name suggests the best seating is outdoors, on a second-floor deck overlooking Ganges Harbour. Highlights of the dependable

**Eats** ●
Al Fresco, **8**
Crescent Moon, **3**
House Piccolo, **4**
Moby's, **2**
Moka House, **5**
Purple Parrot, **7**
Salt Spring
Roasting Co., **6**
Vesuvius
Neighborhood
Pub, **1**

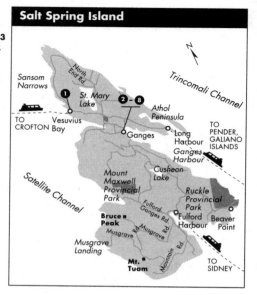

Italian-meets-Pacific Northwest menu include smoked-lamb prosciutto and Asian pasta with shrimp, ginger, garlic, Chinese black beans, and caramelized onions. ⊠ *Grace Point Sq., Ganges Village,* ☎ *250/537–5979.*

$$ ✕ **Moby's.** An ideal place to grab a table and people-watch, this brew pub on the harbor draws the full gamut of grungers, dykes, tourists, backpackers, newlyweds, and older couples. The two-level space has a soaring pitched roof with high windows looking back over the village; a fire roars in the fireplace. The pub food is first-rate and filling; try the crab quesadillas, the breaded halibut burger, or the rich seafood chowder. ⊠ *124 Upper Ganges Rd., Ganges Village,* ☎ *250/ 537–5041.*

$–$$ ✕ **Purple Parrot.** What seems like a simple, albeit cute, luncheonette specializes in spicy Caribbean and Cajun food—fried oysters, blackened snapper, Jamaica jerk chicken, and the like. The Parrot is the gayest eatery in town (and thus among the least touristy). With so few social spots on the island, it's a good place for single travelers, especially women, to connect with the community. ⊠ *170 Fulford–Ganges Rd., Ganges Village,* ☎ *250/537–2204.*

**$–$$** ✕ **Vesuvius Neighborhood Pub.** From the shellacked tables of this friendly little pub on the west side of the island you can watch locals playing darts, admire the fireplace, listen to live music on many nights, or just stare out at the gorgeous bay (which glows a fiery orange and yellow at sunset). The menu is ordinary, but the food—sandwiches, hummus, snow crab, and nachos—is well prepared. ⊠ *By the ferry terminal, 805 Vesuvius Bay Rd., Vesuvius,* ☎ *250/537–2312.*

**$** ✕ **Crescent Moon.** Small, cheap, and sunny, this cafeteria-style eatery serves 10 hot vegetarian dishes (such as tofu in peanut curry) and several cold ones daily. For dessert there are wheat-free organic cookies and brownies. You can enjoy your meal on a cheerful deck outside. Strong dyke following. ⊠ *Corner of Jackson and Hereford Aves., Ganges Village,* ☎ *250/537–1960. No credit cards.*

# Coffeehouse Culture

Victoria and Salt Spring Island have busy, artsy coffeehouses—a bit of a revelation considering the staid reputation of the one and the remoteness of the other. This just goes to show the importance of caffeinated brews throughout the Pacific Northwest. The following java joints aren't explicitly queer, but you can expect to meet kindred souls.

## Victoria

**The Java.** As queer as coffeehouses get in this town, the Java draws an even mix of chess players, crossword solvers, and chatty Cathys. Shops and Inner Harbour attractions are steps away, meaning that plenty of tourists stumble in here, too. ⊠ *537 Johnson St.,* ☎ *250/381–2326.*

**Q Cafe.** On the edge of Victoria's small but dense Chinatown, the Q serves cheap if ordinary food 24 hours a day, along with a nice selection of coffees and desserts. The crowd definitely leans toward the alternative. Bar queens head here after the clubs close. ⊠ *1701 Government St.,* ☎ *250/384–8831.*

## Salt Spring Island

**Moka House.** This swank little coffeehouse in the heart of Ganges Village has yummy hazelnut lattes, bagels, teas, and baked goods. The porch looks across the street toward the harbor. ⊠ *110 Lower Ganges Rd., Ganges Village,* ☎ *250/537–1216.*

**Salt Spring Roasting Co.** Across from Moka, this snazzy storefront has the town's best variety of coffees and teas, plus light sandwiches, quiche, and desserts. Contemporary art lines the walls. The crowd is crunchy and laid-back. ⊠ *109 McPhillips Ave., Ganges Village,* ☎ *250/537–0825.*

# SCENES

## Victoria

Victoria may be the only place on Vancouver Island with gay clubs, but it by no means has a lively nightlife. The two clubs are fine for tourists, but locals are far from thrilled with their options and complain that the scene is incestuous and cliquey.

PRIME SUSPECTS

**B.J.'s.** This dark but expansive basement video lounge has dozens of TV screens, a few dozen cocktail tables, and patrons who take their darts and pool seriously. The space is fairly cruisy. ⊠ *642 Johnson St.,* ☎ *250/388–0505. Crowd: 70/30 m/f, a few straights, all ages, laid-back, mostly local except in summer and during weekends, when tourists make up more than half the crowd.*

**Rumors.** Locals go to great lengths to support the argument that Rumors or B.J.'s is better than the other. In fact, they're both similar in atmosphere, size, appearance, and crowd—and they're both a bit depressing and dated-looking. Rumors is dark, plays loud dance music, has plenty of lounge space, and is in a basement—like its competitor. There's a small dance floor toward the back of the bar and—score one for Rumors—it's open an hour later than B.J.'s. ⊠ *1325 Government St.,* ☎ *250/385–0566. Crowd: similar to B.J.'s, but with a little more attitude; a slightly younger bunch, and more straights on weekends.*

## Salt Spring Island

Ganges is getting more commercial, but there will probably never be much of a nightlife. Anytime you're among a crowd of people on Salt Spring Island, you're likely to be in the company of at least a few queers—odds are strong that they're women, who supposedly outnumber gay men 10 to 1. In either case, singles are few and far between. Overall, the population is an eclectic one—from macho loggers to transplanted urban dwellers to restless alternateens with backpacks.

Social opportunities consist mostly of dining out (try Moby's at night or the Purple Parrot during the day for optimum homo sightings), grabbing a cup of java at either of the two coffeehouses, mingling at the Saturday market, or chatting with folks coming over on the ferry. You can always try picking up hitchhikers, or thumbing around town yourself. This is a common and reasonably safe method of getting around the island, and it's a surefire way to meet folks.

If all else fails, head to Salt Spring Island's one-of-a-kind movie theater inside the old 1898 Central Hall, not far from Vesuvius. The night's feature will be scrawled in chalk outside the front door.

## Action

Victoria's one bathhouse, **Garden Baths** (⊠ 660 Johnson St., ☎ 250/383–6623), is centrally located, but, like the bars mentioned above, not especially busy except during the tourist season.

# SLEEPS

With a major tourist trade and a regular stream of politicians, Victoria has a wealth of hotels, inns, and bed-and-breakfasts. The high-end properties are mostly interchangeable. The one that stands out is the turn-of-the-century Royal Empress, reviewed below. Several B&Bs—mostly unfancy European-style accommodations—cater to a mixed homo/hetero crowd. There often isn't much in the way of amenities—you might not have a phone in your room, or even a private bath—but you can expect a hearty breakfast, a homey atmosphere, and friendly hosts.

The Gulf Islands, like Washington's nearby San Juan Islands, are without major hotel and resort development, although Salt Spring Island has several small motor lodges, most of them dull and not worth your trouble. Better to consider one of the more than 100 bed-and-breakfasts, ranging from rustic homes with one or two rooms sharing a bath to fancy retreats with every creature comfort.

# Victoria

## Hotels

**$$$$**  🏨 **Royal Empress Hotel.** This 1908 Edwardian hostelry is possibly the most desirable place to stay in B.C., and its Empress Room is a fine restaurant. Newer rooms are larger than the original ones yet still in keeping with the hotel's tradition. Celeb spotting is frequent. ⊠ *721 Government St., V8W 1W5,* ☎ *250/384–8111 or 800/441–1414,* 𝔽𝔸𝕏 *250/381–4334. 483 rooms. 5 restaurants, pool, health club.*

**$$–$$$**  🏨 **Swans Hotel.** A former warehouse near Market Square and within walking distance of downtown attractions has been refitted into a distinctive all-suites hotel. Couples traveling together will find Swans a bargain—up to six people can easily fit into its huge rooms. Each has a dining nook, a patio or a terrace, and many have skylights. There's a microbrewery and restaurant on the premises. ⊠ *506 Pandora Ave., V8W 1N6,* ☎ *250/361–3310 or 800/668–7926,* 𝔽𝔸𝕏 *250/ 361–3491. 29 rooms. Restaurant.*

**$**  🏨 **Shamrock Motel.** The dull, squat Shamrock is not especially pretty from the outside, but its staff is warm and hospitable. Clean, cheerful rooms look out over Beacon Hill Park. ⊠ *675 Superior St., V8V 1V1,* ☎ *250/385–8768,* 𝔽𝔸𝕏 *250/ 385–1837. 15 rooms.*

## Guest Houses and Small Hotels

**$$$**  🏨 **Holland House Inn.** Just two blocks from the Inner Harbour and unquestionably one of Victoria's most luxurious small inns, the Holland House doubles as an acclaimed art gallery. Tasteful antiques and original paintings, sculptures, and drawings decorate large and sunny rooms. ⊠ *595 Michigan St., V8V 1S7,* ☎ *250/384–6644,* 𝔽𝔸𝕏 *250/384–6117. 10 rooms with phone, TV, and private bath. Full breakfast. Mixed gay/straight.*

**$$–$$$**  🏨 **Oak Bay Guest House.** Aussie transplants Karl and Jackie Morris bought Oak Bay's only inn a couple of years ago. Their 1912 property in the smart residential neighborhood is about a 10- to 15-minute drive from the Inner Harbour. Smallish but clean rooms all have simple furnishings, floral wallpapering, and modern baths. ⊠ *1052 Newport Ave., V85 5E3,* ☎ *250/598–3812 or 800/575–3812,* 𝔽𝔸𝕏 *250/598–0369. 11 rooms with private bath. Full breakfast. Mostly straight.*

**$–$$**  🏨 **The Weekender.** This contemporary, slightly upscale town house off Dallas Road in the Fairfield neighborhood has three clean and comfortable rooms, one with a sundeck and an ocean view. Innkeeper Michael Maglio generally leaves guests to their own devices, which makes his the perfect place for couples seeking privacy. ⊠ *10 Eberts St., V8S 5L6, ☎ 250/389–1688. 3 rooms with private bath. Continental breakfast. Mostly mixed gay male/lesbian.*

$ 🏠 **The Back Hills.** So named for its location in the Metchosin Hills, an easy and eye-pleasing half-hour drive from the Inner Harbour, this rustic women's retreat makes an ideal starting point for the many outdoor activities in the region. Trails on the 11-acre property yield views of the Olympic mountain range. Guests have the run of the top floor of the house and use of a common kitchen. ⊠ *4470 Leefield Rd., V9C 3Y2, ☎ 250/478–9648. 3 rooms share 2 baths. Full breakfast. Mostly lesbian.*

$ 🏠 **Claddagh House.** Maggie Thompson, whose B&B is not far from downtown and Oak Bay with her young daughter, treats her lodgers like old friends, gladly dispensing tips about local dining, shopping, and touring. Rooms in her 1913 house are simple but warmly appointed. The traditional Irish breakfast keeps many guests energized until dinner. Reflexology and massage are offered at an additional charge. ⊠ *1761 Lee Ave., V8R 4W7, ☎ 250/370–2816, ℻ 250/592–0228. 3 rooms with private bath. Full breakfast. Mixed gay/straight.*

$ 🏠 **Crow's Nest.** One of the most gay-friendly of Victoria's straight-owned properties is a 1911 home with Craftsman (or, as the style is known in these parts, American Chalet) details. It's a stone's throw from Dallas Road and a short walk from Beacon Hill Park. Rooms are decorated with no particular theme—just a mix of antiques and bric-a-brac. They've got plenty of character, even if they're not the fanciest digs in town. A sweet old sheltie and several cats help hosts Kit and Dene greet the guests. ⊠ *71 Linden Ave., V8V 4C9, ☎ 250/383–4492, ℻ 250/383–3140. 3 rooms, 1 with private bath. Full breakfast. Mostly straight.*

## Salt Spring Island

In addition to the properties listed below the **Salt Spring Centre** (⊠ 355 Blackburn Rd., V8K 2B8, ☎ 250/537–2326), a conference facility set on 69 acres of rolling meadows and wooded forest, sponsors self-discovery workshops and other gatherings throughout the year, including women's weekends

at least eight times annually and yoga retreats that are open
to both men and women. The facility is popular among lesbians and gay men. Guests share rooms, which are rented
on a daily, weekly, or monthly basis. If these programs or this
atmosphere interests you, give them a call—even if no workshops are scheduled when you plan to come, you may still
be able to find inexpensive accommodations.

## Guest Houses and Small Hotels

**$$$$**  ☷ **Hastings House.** Salt Spring Island is home to one luxury
property; in fact, this is one of the most exclusive small hotels in the country, with sky-high rates to prove it. The compound consists of five restored farm buildings (including an
especially romantic barn), each containing from two to four
suites. Typical furnishings include hulking stone fireplaces and
museum-quality antiques. Staying here is a rather formal
experience, but if you seek the best of the best, Hastings is
for you. ⊠ *160 Upper Ganges Rd., V8K 2S2,* ☎ *250/537–
2362 or 800/661–9255,* ℻ *250/537–5333. 12 suites with
phone, TV, and private bath. Full breakfast. Mostly straight.*

**$$**  ☷ **Green Rose.** Owners Ron Aird and Tom Hoff have turned
this 1916 farmhouse on 17 acres of rolling fields, orchards,
and flower beds into a delightful country inn with antiques-
filled rooms. You can't beat the setting, which is ideal for cou-
ples seeking a romantic retreat but unable to afford the
Hastings House. A bit north of Ganges, but only a short bike
ride or 25-minute walk. ⊠ *346 Robinson Rd., V8K 1P7,* ☎
*250/537–9927. 3 rooms with private bath. Full breakfast.
Mixed gay/straight.*

**$–$$**  ☷ **Summerhill.** Right up the street from a picturesque egg farm
and minutes from Vesuvius, this contemporary hilltop house
has stunning views of Sansum Narrows. Rooms are bright
and modern, with upscale furnishings. There's plenty of deck
space, gardens, and shaded seating areas, allowing guests to
take full advantage of the wondrous surroundings. ⊠ *209
Chu-an Dr., V8K 1H9,* ☎ *250/537–2727,* ℻ *250/537–
4301. 3 rooms with private bath. Full breakfast. Mostly
mixed gay male/lesbian.*

**$–$$**  ☷ **Villa Valmont.** This replica of a 16th-century French
manor house, complete with a medieval-inspired turret, is nes-
tled amid a 5-acre thicket of trees and thick foliage—you won't
find a more unusual setting on the entire island. Rooms are
small but cozy, with a tasteful mix of antiques and newer

pieces. Despite the extraordinary exterior of the house, Villa Valmont is informal, unfancy, and affordable. ⊠ *140 Kitchen Rd., V8K 2B3,* ☎ *250/653–9232. 3 rooms share 2 baths. Full breakfast. Mixed gay/straight.*

$ 🏨 **Blue Ewe.** Home to some of the friendliest dogs, ducks, goats, sheep, bunnies, and potbelly pigs in North America, the Blue Ewe is run by two exceedingly friendly humans (Bill and Lorcan), who will answer your questions about the island and to steer you toward good restaurants, shops, and outdoor adventures. Their house is high on a forested hill overlooking the water; rooms are colorful and warm, with plenty of sunlight. The common room downstairs is an ideal place to curl up with a book and chat with guests, and with permission you can store food in the fridge or use the kitchen to make lunch or dinner. There's ocean or lake swimming a half mile away in either direction, and a Jacuzzi just outside. ⊠ *1207 Beddis Rd., V8K 1X3,* ☎ *250/537–9344. 3 rooms, 1 with private bath. Hot tub. Full breakfast. Mostly mixed gay male/lesbian.*

$ 🏨 **Fulford Inn.** This homey Tudor-style inn near the Fulford Harbour ferry terminal has modest rooms, a lively pub and restaurant, and a laid-back staff. Though it's not very gay, if you're looking for a motel-style accommodation, this is one of your least expensive options. ⊠ *2661 Fulford–Ganges Rd., V0S 1C0,* ☎ *250/653–4432. 7 rooms with TV and private bath. Restaurant. Mostly straight.*

$ 🏨 **Sunny Side Up.** Water views are abundant from this house on 6 bluff-top acres not far from Fulford Harbour near Ruckle park. Rooms have rustic appointments. ⊠ *120 Andrew Pl., V8K 1X3,* ☎ *250/653–4889. 3 rooms. Hot tub. Full breakfast. Mostly mixed gay male/lesbian.*

# Galiano Island

## Guest Houses and Small Hotels

$$ 🏨 **Bellhouse Inn.** This historic 1890s farmhouse sits on 6 waterfront acres overlooking Bellhouse Bay. Rooms have antiques, brass beds, original fir floors, and Persian rugs, and the owners go to great lengths to make their guests feel at home. From the 300-foot beach you can watch the eagles and killer whales common to the Gulf Islands. ⊠ *29 Farmhouse Rd., Box 16, Site 4, V0N 1P0,* ☎ *250/539–5667 or 800/*

970–7464, FAX 250/539–5316. *4 rooms with private bath. Full breakfast. Mixed gay/straight.*

**$$**  🏠 **Moonshadows Guest House.** Sunlight fills this airy contemporary house whose rooms have grand views of an undulating field with horses and a pond. Of the three rooms, the downstairs suite is the largest, with its own covered deck, massive windows, and a whirlpool bath. The two rooms upstairs are also spacious. ⊠ *771 Georgeson Bay Rd., Galiano Island, V0N 1P0,* ☎ *250/539–5544. 3 rooms with phone and private bath, 2 with TV, hot tub. Full breakfast. Mixed gay/straight.*

# THE LITTLE BLACK BOOK

## At Your Fingertips

**Galiano Chamber of Commerce** (⊠ Box 73, Galiano Island, V0N 1P0, ☎ 250/539–2233). **Lesbian, Gay, Bisexual Alliance of University of Victoria** (☎ 250/472–6395). **Mayne Island Chamber of Commerce** (⊠ General Delivery, Mayne Island, V0N 2J0, no phone). **Salt Spring Island Chamber of Commerce** (⊠ 121 Lower Ganges Rd., V8K 2T1, ☎ 250/537–5252). **Tourism Association of Vancouver Island** (⊠ 302–45 Bastion Sq., Victoria V8W 1J1, ☎ 250/382–3551). **Tourism Victoria's Travel Infocentre** (⊠ 710–1175 Douglas St., V8W 2E1, ☎ 250/382–2160 or, for help with hotel reservations, 800/663–3883). **Tourism Victoria's visitor center** (⊠ 812 Wharf St., ☎ 250/953–2033).

## Gay Media

Victoria has neither a lesbigay bookstore nor a newspaper. Most queers here pick up gay B.C. news from Vancouver's **Xtra West** (☎ 604/684–9696), though it has little coverage of nightlife and events in Victoria. The handy **Island Tides** (☎ 250/629–3660) keeps tabs on the Southern Gulf Islands, and—as the name suggests—has a complete list of island tides; there's no lesbigay coverage. You can also find fairly comprehensive tourist information in the free **Gulf Islander** (☎ 250/537–9933), an annual guide published by the islands' main newspaper, **Driftwood**.

### BOOKSTORES

The nonprofit **Every Woman's Books** (⊠ 635 Johnson St., ☎ 250/388–9411) stocks many lesbian and feminist titles and is also an excellent place for women, regardless of sexual orientation, to find out what's going on throughout the island. Victoria has an outstanding general independent bookstore, **Munroe's** (⊠ 1108 Government St., ☎ 250/382–2464), with a strong queer section. On Salt Spring Island, **Volume II Bookstore** (⊠ Mouat's Mall, Ganges Village, ☎ 250/537–9223), a tiny independent general store, carries maps and books on the region.

## Working Out

There are no specifically or even predominantly gay gyms in Victoria. **Fitness World** (⊠ 3301 Douglas St., ☎ 250/475–6002) is a large, well-equipped downtown gym that's popular with locals and tourists. The **Oak Bay Recreation Center** (⊠ 1975 B St., Oak Bay, ☎ 250/595–7946), a 15-minute drive from the Inner Harbour, is great for swimming, weights, and aerobics. It's open from 6 AM until 1 AM.

# 5 Out in Portland

**Y**OU HAVE TO ADMIRE PORTLAND AND ITS RESIDENTS, few of whom seem to have the slightest interest in turning their city into a huge metropolis. While other American cities grew horizontally and vertically, Portland created massive greenbelts within a couple of miles of the city center and instituted height restrictions on downtown structures.

Since the hippie-dippie '60s, civic leaders have been obsessed with land use. Portlanders capped the number of parking spaces downtown—it's almost impossible to obtain permits to put up a new garage. Then there's the issue of freeways. Back in the early '50s when Robert Moses, the wizard of urban design from back East, paid a visit, locals asked him how to improve their town. Moses suggested tearing down the outmoded wharves and factories fringing the Willamette River to make room for an elevated highway. City planners complied, but decades later their successors realized the folly of this hunk of concrete, tore it down, and replaced it with the Tom McCall Waterfront Park (*see* Downtown, *below*).

Portland and Seattle once looked and felt similar. Each existed on an intimate scale, wore a fairly old-fashioned facade, and contained a maze of seedy downtown streets. Though urban renewal has softened Portland's rougher edges, the city's scale hasn't changed. Its rows of cast-iron dinosaurs are interrupted occasionally by gleaming glass-and-concrete towers, but none is higher than 36 stories and only a handful are higher than 20. Portland's neighbor to the north, meanwhile, has actively sought international status. In many ways Seattle's expansion is impressive—though it has grown tremendously it's still a green city with a strong environmental record and much to recommend it. But few Portlanders would trade their unflashy, insular world for Seattle's. In greater Portland you'll find more than 1.6 million people perfectly content with small-town living.

More than 1.6 million people? Small-town living? A paradox, you say? In some ways Portlanders are forced to accept at least small-*city* living. For all its parks and greenery, downtown is an urban space. But it's one with a human feel, with a grassy 12-block central boulevard, several largely intact historic districts, and built-in growth restrictions—there's a river on one side and mountains on the other three.

Bordering Portland's commercial sections and just a short walk away are residential neighborhoods such as the Northwest that look not the slightest bit urban. Across the river Portland sprawls for miles to the east. Many of the several dozen communities here look alike from an automobile window, but if you get out and walk around you'll discern their distinct personalities, ethnic makeups, and styles of architecture.

Portland doesn't have a gay quarter, but just about every section of town has a smattering of homo households. Many queerfolk live in the Northwest (sometimes called Nob Hill). A slightly more bohemian and more lesbian contingent resides in Hawthorne in the southeast. Others have discovered the charms of Broadway and the Hollywood district in the northeast. But these are not predominately gay areas.

Counterculturists have long been attracted to the seclusion, serenity, and rugged individualism of Oregon in general and Portland in particular. But the small-town mentality has also fostered distrust of outsiders. Portlanders act—and react—from a gut level, uninfluenced by external forces. You will have little success imposing your beliefs on the people of this city: Liberals can't be told to soften their views or moderate their opinions; conservatives are equally inflexible.

This means that homosexuals and ethnic minorities in Portland find themselves in a precarious position. They possess strength in numbers and sympathy from many politicians. But local hatemongers such as white supremacist Tom Metzger and homophobe Lon Mabon have found secure and visible platforms from which to spew their bile. In the 1990s Mabon (who ran unsuccessfully in 1996 in the Republican primary for the U.S. Senate) and his group the Oregon Citizen's Alliance sponsored ballot initiatives and other antigay activities. In response, lesbians and gays founded Basic Rights

Oregon, which has become one of the most successful statewide civil-rights organizations in the country.

Since the first ballot initiative (Measure 13) appeared, similar campaigns waged in Oregon have failed in popular elections. Basic Rights Oregon's counterattacks have helped defeat these measures, if only by slim margins. Portland itself is an extremely tolerant city whose general population largely rejects the propaganda of the Oregon Citizen's Alliance; nevertheless, one does see random acts of intolerance.

Portland is the sort of city where someone like Kevin Kelly Keith can be seen in a pickup truck outfitted with placards bearing antiqueer slogans. He parks his four-wheel pulpit in high-profile areas and sits in a chair mounted on the roof, overseeing the discomfort and anger he provokes. Of course, Portland is also home to defiant people like Billie Lou Kahn. When Ms. Kahn, a 52-year-old lesbian, stumbled upon the controversial pickup truck, she ran inside a nearby variety store, bought a can of black spray paint, and covered Mr. Keith's hateful signs with a message of her own: "Ignorance Kills."

# THE LAY OF THE LAND

The heart of Portland lies just below the confluence of the Columbia and the Willamette (pronounced wuh-*lamm*-ett) rivers. The Columbia is the border between Washington and Oregon; from it, the Willamette twists in a southerly direction, bisecting the city center. Portland is divided into four quadrants; the Willamette being the north–south spine and Burnside Street being the east–west spine.

Portland's commercial core is in the southwest, near Burnside Street and the river. The northwest quadrant is also heavily developed near the river. Both sections contain Portland's oldest neighborhoods, and both give way to steep, posh suburban hills outside the city center. Across the river the terrain is flat, the streets gridlike for miles, the homes and businesses newer, the population mostly lower and middle class. Though there's less to do east of the river, visitors to Portland will find good reasons to explore both sides.

## Downtown

Portland has an eye-pleasing, though unspectacular, downtown. The skyline is varied in height, color, and shape, and blocks are small. The bases of all buildings are built out to the sidewalk, and their ground floors are required to have display windows. High-end boutiques border pawn shops, trattorias sit beside burger joints, and postmodern boxes rise above cast-iron Victorians. For 12 blocks Park Avenue (a.k.a. "the Park Blocks") is marked by a green median of century-old trees—this breadth of nature was established in 1852, early evidence of Portland's appreciation for its natural resources. The city center is a planner's dream, a bona fide neighborhood with several fountains, some parks, and an abundance of statuary. The streets are busy with nine-to-fivers all day, and they remain lively into the evening when a flood of teens, genXers, and thirtysomethings descends upon music clubs, cafés, and coffeehouses.

Downtown's boundary is perfectly clear: Burnside Street to the north, the river to the east, and curving I–405 to the south and west. Along the river the **Tom McCall Waterfront Park** stretches for more than a mile, providing a scenic venue for cycling, jogging, blading, and sunning. Concert series and Rose Festival events (*see* When to Go, *below*) take place here. The park begins north of the **Oregon Maritime Museum** (⌗ 113 S.W. Front Ave., ☎ 503/224–7724), where exhibits and tours of a restored sternwheeler celebrate Portland's history as one of the West Coast's foremost shipping centers. McCall park terminates at the **RiverPlace Promenade,** a contemporary condo and shopping complex. From the Promenade you can walk across the Hawthorne Bridge to reach the kids-infested **Oregon Museum of Science and Industry** (⌗ 1945 S.E. Water Ave., ☎ 503/797–4000), a hands-on center of technological discovery with a planetarium, an Omnimax theater, a retired military submarine, and scientific exhibits.

Back across the bridge on the west side of the Willamette the six-block **Yamhill Historic District,** a rectangle of classic Italianate cast-iron buildings that date from the early 1870s, runs from about Taylor Street to Morrison Street close to the waterfront.

Brown baggers spend lunch hour at **Pioneer Square,** a tidy redbrick plaza at the intersection of Yamhill Street and Broadway. Many high-end chain stores are clustered here. **Niketown** (⌗ 930 S.W. 6th Ave., ☎ 503/221–6453) is the unabashedly commercial tribute to the Portland-based maker of athletic wear. The downtown branch of the upscale **Nordstrom** (⌗ 701 S.W. Broadway, ☎ 503/224–6666) department store can be rather cruisy. The indoor **Galleria** (✉ 921 S.W. Morrison St., ☎ 503/228–2748) mall has 50 stores. **Pioneer Place** (✉ 700 S.W. 5th Ave., ☎ 503/228–5800), also an indoor mall, has 70.

South of Pioneer Square the **Portland Center for the Performing Arts** (✉ S.W. Broadway and S.W. Main St., ☎ 503/796–9293) is one of the West Coast's most impressive such facilities, with four theaters, a lecture series, and concert halls presenting ballet, opera, and classical music. The **Portland Art Museum** (✉ 1219 S.W. Park Ave., ☎ 503/226–2811) specializes in Native American, regional contemporary, and graphic arts and has a generous representation of traditional Asian, European, and American masterworks. The **Oregon Historical Center** (✉ 1200 S.W. Park Ave., ☎ 503/306–5198) has changing and permanent exhibits documenting the history of the Pacific Northwest, as well as a renowned research library. This neighborhood takes in much of the campus of **Portland State University,** hence the high number of students milling about.

North of Pioneer Square, bounded by 4th and 11th avenues and Oak and Yamhill streets, is the **Glazed Terra-Cotta Historic District,** worth a visit for architecture buffs. Run your eye across the rooflines of these early 20th-century buildings and you'll notice ornate griffins, floral displays, and animal heads.

## The Pearl District and Stark Street

The warehouses and defunct railyards of the **Pearl District,** the center of which is a few blocks east of I–405, north of Burnside Street to about Hoyt Street, are rapidly being developed into condos and businesses.

On the south side of Burnside Street lies the city's tiny gay entertainment mecca, the commercial spine of which is **Stark Street.** Though bar-studded Stark Street is slightly seedy—it recalls San Francisco's Polk Street—it's generally safe and is a short walk from most major downtown hotels and the many restaurants and boutiques in northwest Portland. Vintage-clothing, used-record, and book shops line Burnside and Oak streets. Famous **Powell's City of Books** (✉ 1005 W. Burnside St., ☎ 503/228–4651), with new and used titles, takes up a full block. The store's Anne Hughes Coffee Room is a great place for lattes and butter cookies—and a fine spot for cerebral cruising.

The neighborhood's malty smell comes from the **Blitz-Weinhard Brewing Co.** (⊠ 1133 W. Burnside St., ☎ 503/222–4351), producers of a fine local beer. Begun 130 years ago by Henry Weinhard, the brewery shows no signs of slowing down; tours are available Monday through Friday at noon, 1:30, and 3 PM. The Stark Street area hasn't many attractions unless you're an Elvis fan, in which case a visit to the bizarre 24-hour **Church of Elvis** (⊠ 720 S.W. Ankeny St., ☎ 503/226–3671) is a must. Hours vary, but many days you can drop by this sanctuary to listen to a sermon, take part in a legal wedding, or pose for a photo with an Elvis look-alike.

## Old Town

The oldest commercial part of town begins with the **Skidmore Historic District,** in the blocks immediately south and west of the Burnside Bridge. Buildings are a mix of cast iron and glazed terra-cotta, and though many are restored, the area retains a skid-row atmosphere. You'll find music clubs, restaurants, and galleries here. The dramatic **Skidmore Fountain** (⊠ Ankeny St., just in from Front St.), with its granite troughs and carved lion-head spouts, dates from 1888 and the days of transportation by horse. From March through December the square surrounding the fountain is the site of the **Portland Saturday Market** (⊠ 108 W. Burnside St., ☎ 503/222–6072), where (on Saturday and Sunday) more than 300 vendors sell arts and crafts, junk, collectibles, and food.

Continue north above Burnside to reach Old Town's many restaurants and several divey gay bars. This neighborhood is in a state of transition, as is **Chinatown** just to the west; the latter's ceremonial gate stands at the intersection of Northwest 4th Avenue and Burnside Street.

## Northwest

Though it's devoid of gay bars, Portland's **Northwest** is one of city's prime spots for gay eats and shopping. Technically called (though only occasionally referred to as) Nob Hill and named in the 1880s for the eponymous San Francisco neighborhood, Portland's version isn't anywhere near as posh, but has some fine Victorian houses. **Northwest 23rd** and **Northwest 21st avenues** are the area's two commercial strips. Both, from about Burnside north to around Thurman Street, are replete with alternative-minded students, yuppies, gay men, lesbians, feminists, and aging hippies. Twenty-third Avenue is more upscale, but 21st has the better restaurants.

## Southwest

Southwestern Portland is a hilly neighborhood of twisting roads and Colonial Revival mansions that are among the most valuable real estate in the city. At ¹,000 feet above sea level, **Council Crest Park** is the highest point within the city limits. The panoramic view takes in everything from the downtown skyline to Mt. St. Helens in the distance. The green lawn is a wonderful place to lie in the sun. The drive to Council Crest involves many different streets; it's best to consult a map. From downtown begin by following Southwest 12th Avenue into the foothills and keep winding upward.

West of downtown via U.S. 26, the city's century-old **Washington Park Zoo** (✉ 4001 S.W. Canyon Rd., ☎ 503/226–7627) sits in the middle of 322-acre **Washington Park,** which is crisscrossed by several trails so wooded you'd never know you're only a couple of miles from the city center. Near the zoo the **World Forestry Center** (✉ 4033 S.W. Canyon Rd., ☎ 503/228–1367) dedicates itself to educating the public about the preservation and management of forests around the globe; it contains a re-created Central African rain forest and old-growth forests of the Pacific Northwest. On the opposite side of the park, and reached via Burnside Street, sits the **International Rose Test Garden** (✉ 400 S.W. Kingston Ave., ☎ 503/823–3636); 10,000 bushes with more than 500 varieties are displayed within its 4 acres. Portland is nicknamed the City of Roses, owing to the floral beauty produced by its mild climate. Since 1907 the town's premier must-attend affair has been the Rose Festival (*see* When to Go, *below*). Just above the test garden is a 5½-acre **Japanese Garden** (✉ 611 S.W. Kingston Ave., ☎ 503/223–4070). Portlanders all seem obsessed with gardening, so it's no surprise that these five distinctive Japanese-style gardens (including tea, strolling pond, moss, sand-and-stone, and flat varieties) are among the most impressive outside Asia.

Another attraction near Washington Park is the **Pittock Mansion** (✉ 3229 N.W. Pittock Dr., ☎ 503/823–3624), a restored French Renaissance–inspired home filled with art and antiques and set on 46 wooded acres. Many a queen has feasted on the elegant afternoon tea presented in the Gate Lodge Restaurant inside the Pittock's old caretaker's cottage. The grounds abut the largest wooded municipal preserve in the country, the 5,000-acre **Forest Park.** You can bike or hike along 70 miles of trails, where you may spot one of the park's many black bear and elk.

## The Lloyd District and Northeast Broadway

Once a derelict industrial neighborhood on the northeastern shores of the Willamette River, the **Lloyd District** is now Portland's postindustrial homage to mall and convention culture. Anchored by the twin-towered **Oregon Convention Center** and the 20,000-seat **Rose Garden Arena** (home to the Trail Blazers pro-basketball team), the Lloyd District isn't much of strolling neighborhood, but nonetheless receives a good bit of foot traffic. If you're not here for a game or a business function, you may still wish to pop over for some high-intensity shopping at the 200-store **Lloyd Center** (✉ 2201 Lloyd Center, off N.E. Multnomah St., ☎ 503/282–2511), a sprawling supermall east of the convention center.

From here you're a short walk from the **Northeast Broadway** neighborhood. This swiftly emerging business district has deep roots in the queer community. Most of the action is along Broadway from about 18th Avenue to 28th Avenue. One recent arrival is **Gai-Pied** (*see* Bookstores, *below*), the city's first gay bookstore.

Continue east to reach the Hollywood District, where there are restaurants and shops, including a huge antiques emporium, the **New Antique Village Mall** (✉ 1969 N.E. 42nd Ave., ☎ 503/288–1051).

A couple of miles to the northeast lies one of the region's most unusual attractions, the 62-acre **Grotto** (✉ N.E. 85th Ave. and Sandy Blvd., ☎ 503/254–7371), a tranquil parcel of fir trees and lush trails. You can take an elevator to the top of a 130-foot cliff to meditate in the interdenominational **Marilyn Moyer Chapel** and take in views of Mt. St. Helens and the Cascade mountain range.

## Hawthorne and Sellwood

Though Portland is not as visibly gay a city as Seattle or San Francisco, it has one of America's strongest feminist and lesbian communities. The **Hawthorne District** in the southeast quadrant is the most concentrated lesbian enclave, but it's home as well to countless liberal-minded sorts. Both **Southeast Stark** and **Southeast Belmont streets,** which run north of the Hawthorne District, hold a share of the area's coffeehouses, boutiques, and music clubs. But the main commercial stretch is **Hawthorne Boulevard,** which first becomes interesting around 15th Avenue, peaks in funkiness between 30th and 40th avenues, and quiets down above 50th Avenue. A grittier version of Nob Hill, the Hawthorne District is a great place for Sunday brunch, browsing in bookshops and galleries, and listening to poetry readings and folk bands while sipping your coffee. You can catch queer performance and entertainment at the **Echo Theatre** (✉ 1515 S.E. 37th Ave., ☎ 503/231–1232) and the highly avant-garde **Stark Raving Theatre** (✉ 4319 S.E. Hawthorne Blvd., ☎ 503/232–7072). The nearby **Baghdad Theater** (✉ 3702 S.E. Hawthorne Blvd., ☎ 503/230–0895) is a trendy pub-cum-cinema.

Take Route 99E south for several miles to reach the **Old Sellwood Antique Row;** it runs along **Southeast 13th Street,** between Bidwell and Sherrett streets. This community of wood-frame Victorians was annexed by Portland in 1893 and contains more than 50 great antiques shops.

## Salem

Oregon's capital city, which is less than an hour's drive south of Portland, draws relatively few tourists, but you will find enough here to keep you busy for a day or two. This city of 100,000 has several historic districts with examples of 19th-century industrial and residential architecture. Contact the **Salem Convention and Visitors Bureau** (✉ 1313 Mill St. SE, Salem 97301, ☎ 503/581–4325 or 800/874–7012) for information on the region.

Salem doesn't have a whole lot to offer in the way of queer entertainment but has a friendly gay bar, Sneakers (*see* Scenes, *below*). **Rosebud & Fish** (✉ 524 State St., ☎ 503/399–9960) has a great selection of lesbigay and feminist books.

# GETTING AROUND

A section comprising downtown, up to Hoyt Street and then bound by I–405 and the Willamette River, is known as Fareless Square in transit lingo: Within this 300-square-block area, **Tri-Met** (☎ 503/238–7433) bus, restored trolley, and MAX light-rail travel are free; outside it, public transportation is still affordable. And for $1, you can hit about a dozen of the city's top attractions by riding the **ART Bus** (Bus 63), which you can pick up at the Downtown Visitor Information Center at Salmon Street and Front Avenue. Though Portland's mass transit system is efficient and user-friendly, visitors have little reason to use it because navigating downtown streets is not difficult and attractions here and on Nob Hill are mostly within walking distance. You'll probably need a car to get to the southwestern hills, Northeast Broadway, and the Hawthorne District.

Taxis from Portland International Airport (PDX) to downtown hotels cost $25, **Raz Transportation** (☎ 503/246–4676) buses about $8.50. Or take the **Tri-Met** (☎ 503/238–7433) Bus 12, a 40-minute ride, for just over a dollar.

# WHEN TO GO

Portland's most famous event, the **Rose Festival and Grand Floral Parade** (☎ 503/227–2681) is immensely popular with the queer community. Events are held throughout June, with the parade usually the first weekend. Gayfolk, usually clad in white gloves, hang out in front of Nordstrom to cheer on those drag queens marching in the procession.

The city's late-June **gay pride celebration** (☎ 503/295–9788) includes a parade, a rally, and parties at local bars. The first Sunday after gay pride is **Peacock in the Park** (☎ 503/284–1733), a Wigstock-like dress-up event in Washington Park that raises scholarship money for young lesbians and gay men.

In late October the Imperial Sovereign Rose Court (a local queer fund-raising organization) holds its annual **Coronation Ball.** Many cities have similar courts, but Portland's is one of the most active and lively—this drag extravaganza is a great deal of fun, and people come from all over the Pacific Northwest to attend. Call the folks at the Embers (*see* Scenes, *below*) for details.

# EATS

Portland's dining scene may not be flashy, but it is diverse. Immigration from Asian countries is as common here as it is in other West Coast cities, and Portland also has strong

Mexican, Eastern European, German, and Irish communities. The variety is evident in the number of ethnic eateries, and perhaps owing to the abundance of fresh- and saltwater seafood you'll find ample contemporary Pacific Northwest cuisine. If a queer atmosphere is important to you, eat at one of the several gay bars with restaurants—these places are usually affordable, though the food hardly memorable. Virtually all the city's top restaurants are gay-friendly, but none has an extremely gay following.

If you're looking for some food to bring along on a hiking expedition near town or a trip to one of the gay beaches, check out the **Pastaworks** (⊠ 3735 S.E. Hawthorne Blvd., ☎ 503/232–1010; ⊠ 4834 S.E. Division St., ☎ 503/236–1190; ⊠ 735 N.W. 21st Ave., ☎ 503/221–3002) markets, all three of which happen to be in fairly queer neighborhoods.

For price ranges, *see* Chart B at the front of this guide.

## West of the Willamette

$$$–
$$$$
X **The Heathman Restaurant.** In a showcase kitchen at the center of the Heathman dining room, chef Philippe Boulot whips up such masterpieces as boletus-mushroom-dusted swordfish (with potato, coriander confit of carrot, and Amontillado sherry sauce) and roasted Northwest fallow venison wrapped in applewood-smoked bacon with bourbon-glazed acorn squash and huckleberry sauce. A few critics complain of stuffy service, but most agree that Boulot delivers the goods. ⊠ *Heathman Hotel, 1001 S.W. Broadway,* ☎ *503/241–4100.*

$$$–
$$$$
X **Higgins.** Chef Greg Higgins, who headed the prestigious Heathman for more than a decade, opened this intimate celebrity-popular spot near the Oregon Historical Museum. The response to his Mediterranean, Asian, and American cooking (try the grilled red rockfish with a citrus and lime glaze) has been positive, though less uniformly ecstatic than during his Heathman tenure. ⊠ *1239 S.W. Broadway,* ☎ *503/222–9070.*

$$$–
$$$$
X **Wildwood.** One of Portland's hottest purveyors of Pacific Northwest cuisine is typically trendy, with earthy hues, curvy chairs and tables inside, and postmodern metal furniture out on the patio. The menu changes often but has featured such winners as corn-and-saffron soup with roasted-pepper

puree and seared halibut with risotto and Romano beans. The wood-baked mussels with saffron and tomato broth are excellent. ⊠ *1221 N.W. 21st Ave.,* ☎ *503/248–9663.*

**\$\$–\$\$\$** ✕ **Basta's.** Tastee-Freez customers may have once passed through the building that now houses Basta's, but the northwest Portland restaurant cultivates the smart set with pan-fried oysters in a Tuscan verde sauce and delicious specials like Oregon rabbit braised with seasonal vegetables and fresh marjoram. Unbelievably rich and delicious desserts follow. ⊠ *410 N.W. 21st Ave.,* ☎ *503/274–1572.*

**\$\$–\$\$\$** ✕ **Café des Amis.** A romantic and very queer place to take a first date, this elegantly appointed bistro on Nob Hill serves reasonably priced country-French fare—fillet of beef with garlic and port sauce, duck swimming in blackberries, and savory wild-mushroom ravioli. ⊠ *1987 N.W. Kearney St.,* ☎ *503/295–6487.*

**\$\$–\$\$\$** ✕ **Cassidy's.** Power lunchers and moon-eyed lovers have made this old-fashioned restaurant a favorite. The contemporary menu features Pacific Northwest variations on seafood and pasta. Later in the evening actors and stage crews from local theaters stop by for a late meal, drinks, or coffee. ⊠ *1331 S.W. Washington St.,* ☎ *503/223–0054.*

**\$\$–\$\$\$** ✕ **Hobo's.** The city's one upscale gay restaurant is so popular that lots of straight movers and shakers come here, too. With a classy lounge and piano bar the place has the feel of a big gay supper club. The two-level dining room has exposed brick walls and formal white linen—you'll see a lot of suits in here most nights. The menu concentrates on steak and seafood. ⊠ *120 N.W. 3rd Ave.,* ☎ *503/224–3285.*

**\$\$–\$\$\$** ✕ **Papa Haydn.** One of the more yuppified hangouts in northwest Portland is famous for its weekend brunches. For weekday lunches try the overstuffed sandwiches such as Gruyère and Black Forest ham; tasty dinner entrées include chicken marinated in apple brandy. The desserts here never disappoint; many patrons stop by solely for German and Austrian pastries and coffee. At the adjacent Jo Bar & Rotisserie (☎ 503/222–0048), you'll find more formal and expensive fare. ⊠ *701 N.W. 23rd Ave.,* ☎ *503/228–7317; also (without Jo Bar & Rotisserie)* ⊠ *5829 S.E. Milwaukie Ave.,* ☎ *503/232–9440.*

**\$\$–\$\$\$** ✕ **Zefiro's.** The heavy gold curtains, white linen, and black chairs give it the feel of a Shriners Hall, but Zefiro's serves cutting-edge international fare with an emphasis on Mediter-

# Downtown Portland

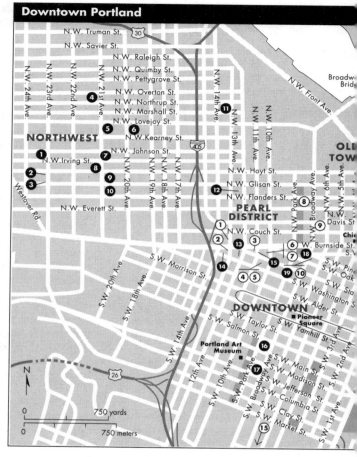

**Eats** ●

Basta's, **10**
Bridgeport Brewing Co., **11**
Café des Amis, **6**
Cassidy's, **14**
Coffee People, **2**
Coffee Time, **7**

Dan & Louis Oyster Bar, **21**
Garbanzo's, **5**
Gypsy Cafe, **8**
Hamburger Mary's, **18**
The Heathman Resaurant, **16**
Higgins, **17**

Hobo's, **20**
Montage, **22**
Old Wives' Tales, **24**
Papa Haydn, **1**
Pizzicato, **3**
Rimsky-Korsakoffee House, **25**

The Roxy, **15**
Saigon Kitchen, **23**
Sauce Box, **19**
Shaker's, **12**
Suriya Thai Cuisine, **13**
Wildwood, **4**
Zefiro's, **9**

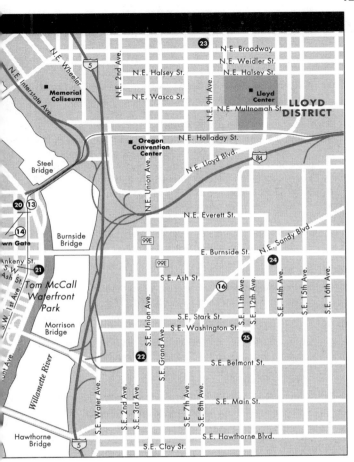

**Scenes** ○

Boxx's/
The Brig, **6**
Candlelight
Room, **15**
C. C.
Slaughter's, **5**
City Nightclub, **1**
Darcelle XV, **12**

Dirty Duck, **11**
Eagle, **2**
Embers, **9**
Fox and
Hound, **14**
Hobo's, **13**
La Luna, **16**
Panorama, **7**

Ray's
Ordinary, **8**
Scandals, **4**
Silverado, **3**
Squeeze Box, **10**

ranean cooking. You can order a traditional Greek salad, but more typical are such exotic dishes as grilled Chinook salmon with Thai tamarind curry, served with jasmine rice and green and yellow beans. ✉ *500 N.W. 21st Ave.,* ☎ *503/226–3394.*

**$$  ✕ Bridgeport Brewing Co.** Microbreweries are a legitimately big whoop in Portland, and this one in a century-old converted warehouse in the northern reaches of the Pearl District (near the Broadway Bridge) is one of the best in town, offering a wide variety of bitters, ales, and stouts. The pizza here is locally revered (the dough, of course, made with unfermented beer) and comes with seasonally changing toppings. The focaccia sandwiches and salads are excellent. ✉ *1313 N.W. Marshall St.,* ☎ *503/241–7179.*

**$–$$  ✕ Gypsy Cafe.** Though the kitschy '50s-diner decor (funky lamps and retro colors) is a bit overdone, the Gypsy serves up great comfort fare. You can order eggs Benedict the usual way or vegetarian, with spinach and tomatoes. There's a narrow, sunny patio off to the side. ✉ *625 N.W. 21st Ave.,* ☎ *503/796–1859.*

**$–$$  ✕ Hamburger Mary's.** It was never all that gay in its old location, and a move next to the Benson Hotel on Broadway has mainstreamed Mary's even further. Which is not necessarily a bad thing. The big rainbow flag in the window of this plant-filled eatery lets the world know that queers are welcome. Burgers and grilled-chicken sandwiches prevail at this always dependable spot for pre-bar-hopping sustenance. ✉ *239 S.W. Broadway,* ☎ *503/223–0900.*

**$–$$  ✕ Sauce Box.** The latest self-consciously hip café to grace downtown Portland delivers tasty multinational fare—veggie samosas, grilled-cheddar-and-tomato sandwiches, quesadillas, Chinese pot stickers—in an austere dining room near the gay entertainment district and several of the historic downtown hotels. Tripping music, a tiny upstairs pool lounge, patrons sporting the latest gas-station-attendant uniforms, and flatware that looks stolen from ValuJet heighten the tortured artiste ambience. ✉ *214 S.W. Broadway,* ☎ *503/241–3393.*

**$  ✕ Dan & Louis Oyster Bar.** This simple fish house in the Skidmore Historic District has been run by the same family since 1919. In addition to the tasty raw oysters, you can sample a rich oyster stew, clam chowder, and several seafood platters. The two dining rooms have simple wood tables, and walls covered with decorative dinner plates. ⊠ *208 S.W. Ankeny St.,* ☎ *503/227–5906.*

$  ✕ **Pizzacato.** This chic little pizzeria's pies are available with any number of toppings. Lamb sausage, prosciutto, and eggplant are a few options; you can also choose from an assortment of focaccia sandwiches. Pizzacato is on a well-trafficked street corner—sit outside on black wrought-iron furniture to enjoy an optimum crowd-ogling experience. ⊠ *505 N.W. 23rd Ave.,* ☎ *503/242–0023;* ⊠ *2811 E. Burnside St.,* ☎ *503/236– 6045.*

$  ✕ **The Roxy.** Gay meets grunge in the queer district's 24-hour study in Formica. On any given night you'll see big hair, pierced extremities, lotsa muscle, leather, rubber, drag, you name it. The Roxy is liveliest after the bars close, so expect a wait. Good sandwiches and egg dishes—a specialty is the Soylent Green omelet (spinach, mushroom, cheddar cheese). ⊠ *1121 S.W. Stark St.,* ☎ *503/223–9160.*

$  **Shaker's.** Several cuts above your average greasy spoon (the generous use of Formica and knotty pine notwithstanding), this très gay Pearl District favorite is justly renowned for its filling breakfasts (Scottish oats, challah French toast) and lunches where burgers reign supreme (the tuna's pretty memorable, too). As the name suggests, hundreds of salt and pepper shakers—enough to suggest a disturbing fanaticism on the part of the owner who collects them—are displayed in glass bookcases throughout. ⊠ *1212 N.W. Glisan St.,* ☎ *503/221–0011. No credit cards.*

$  ✕ **Suriya Thai Cuisine.** This is an extremely inexpensive Thai restaurant around the corner from Stark Street's gay bars. The decor is spare, the curries fiery, and the service friendly. ⊠ *1231 S.W. Washington St.,* ☎ *503/228–5775.*

## East of the Willamette

$$$–  ✕ **Genoa.** The city's most esteemed northern Italian restau-
$$$$  rant has been wowing national culinary magazines since the early 1970s. You may have to work to snag a reservation, especially on weekends (Genoa has only 10 tables), but being queer definitely won't hurt your chances of getting in—the restaurant has long been favored within the community. Seven-course prix-fixe dinners include antipasto, soup, pasta, fish or salad, entrée, dessert, and fruit, so bring a large stomach. This may sound like a sumptuous to-do, but dining here

**128**

**Eats ●**
Bread and Ink Cafe, **13**
Brite Spot, **15**
Cafe Arabesque, **2**
Cafe Lena, **8**
Caprial's Bistro and Wine, **17**
Chez José, **1**
Coffee People, **12**
Common Grounds, **14**
Garbanzo's, **11**
Genoa, **7**
Il Piatto, **5**
La Catalana, **9**
Papa Haydn, **16**
Pizzacato, **4**
28 East, **3**
Utopia, **10**
Wild Abandon, **6**

**Scenes ○**
Bar of the Gods, **4**
Choices, **2**
Joq's, **1**
Starky's, **3**

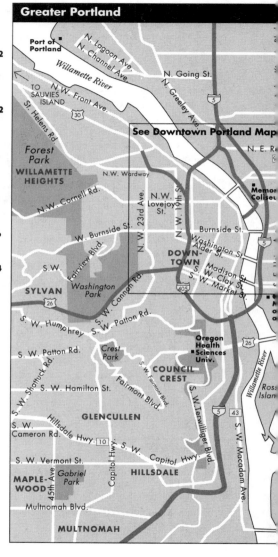

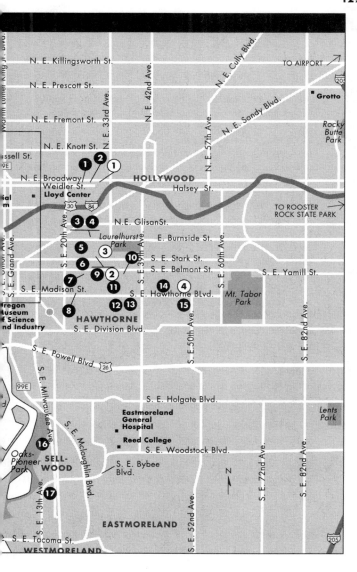

is a relaxing and easygoing event. ✉ *2832 S.E. Belmont St.,* ☎ *503/238–1464.*

**\$\$–\$\$\$** ✕ **Bread and Ink Cafe.** This Hawthorne favorite draws a cerebral crowd for Mediterranean, Mexican, and Yiddish fare (how's that for an unlikely trinity?). The cheeseburgers garner raves all around, as do the chicken enchiladas with a spicy tomatillo salsa, and a filling Yiddish brunch offered Sundays. Check out the freshly baked breads and desserts. ✉ *3610 S.E. Hawthorne Blvd.,* ☎ *503/239–4756.*

**\$\$–\$\$\$** ✕ **Caprial's Bistro and Wine.** Many diners hear about this place from part-owner Caprial Pence's PBS cooking show. Dishes featured on the show highlight the eclectic regional menu: warm spinach salad with dried-cherry dressing, beef tenderloin with arugula pesto, and ginger-peach upside-down cake. ✉ *7015 S.E. Milwaukie Ave.,* ☎ *503/236–6457.*

**\$\$–\$\$\$** ✕ **Il Piatto.** The best of the romantic Italian trattorias on the east side specializes in regional dishes, including sautéed calves liver, a delicious risotto with rock shrimp, oysters, and shellfish, and many varieties of pasta. The country-Italian decor is warm and upbeat, with sponge-painted walls and bottles, jars, jugs, and candlesticks sprinkled liberally about. Consider stopping by late in the evening for dessert and coffee. ✉ *2348 S.E. Ankeny St.,* ☎ *503/236–4997.*

**\$\$–\$\$\$** ✕ **La Catalana.** Hand-painted ceramics and objets d'art fill the gay-frequented La Catalana, one of the most romantic restaurants in eastern Portland. Fresh bass and trout are specialties, as is the appetizer of mussels on the half shell with spinach mousse, and the salad of roasted vegetables and fresh garlic with a sherry vinaigrette. ✉ *2821 S.E. Stark St.,* ☎ *503/232–0948.*

**\$\$–\$\$\$** ✕ **28 East.** Black-metal chandeliers, high ceilings, and yellow and orange tones create a festive and unpretentious atmosphere at this neighborhood bistro whose star is rising rapidly along with the strip of offbeat shops it anchors. Pizzas, grilled sea scallops, and tasty meat, seafood, and poultry grills are menu highlights. ✉ *40 N.E. 28th Ave.,* ☎ *503/235–9060.*

**\$\$** ✕ **Montage.** A teetering redbrick building directly below the Morrison Street Bridge in a slightly dicey warehouse district houses one of Portland's quirkiest taverns. Chic grungers, graying hippies, and artistes congregate for such diverse fare as sautéed sea bass with crabs, biscuits with port sausage, and the kitchen's trademark jambalayas. ✉ *301 S.E. Morrison St.,* ☎ *503/234–1324. No credit cards.*

**\$\$** ✕ **Wild Abandon.** This dark and intimate restaurant, a great place to bring a date, dishes up eclectic cuisine with new American overtones. There's a risotto of the day—a typical one might have house-smoked salmon and mussels with crème fraîche. Grilled beef tenderloin topped with a wild-mushroom demi-glace and a side of garlic mashed potatoes is another favorite. Sunday brunch is popular. ✉ *2411 S.E. Belmont St.,* ☎ *503/232–4458.*

**\$–\$\$** ✕ **Chez José.** You're as likely to find a mom and dad with a zillion children as you are a posse of muscle queens in this cavernous Mexican restaurant with a festive patio out back. Along with the usual south-of-the-border selections, the menu shows off shrimp in a tangy honey-chipotle sauce, and squash enchiladas with a spicy peanut sauce. ✉ *2200 N.E. Broadway,* ☎ *503/280–9888.*

**\$** ✕ **Brite Spot.** The food is filling and fatty, the way it's supposed to be, at this HoJo-esque breakfast and lunch spot in the heart of the Hawthorne District. The attached Space Room is a bizarre, alternateen-infested cocktail lounge with tacky intergalactic murals and lots of Naugahyde. ✉ *4800 S.E. Hawthorne Blvd.,* ☎ *503/235–6957.*

**\$** ✕ **Cafe Arabesque.** Filled with ottomans, sofas, and exotic colors, this small café in the blossoming Northeast Broadway district is one of the city's best dining bargains. Generous helpings of hummus, green salad with feta and tahini dressing, and Syrian flatbread are served, along with chicken gyros, broiled eggplant sandwiches, and falafel. The desserts, among them baklava and *namoura* (a confection of farina, coconut, almonds, and a sugar syrup), are quite fine. ✉ *2432 N.E. Broadway,* ☎ *503/287–3495.*

**\$** ✕ **Garbanzo's.** The Hawthorne branch of this falafel bar has a big dyke following; the Northwest branch is more yuppie-guppie. Both have shaded courtyards and airy dining rooms. Good veggie burgers, hummus, tahini, and salads. ✉ *3433 S.E. Hawthorne Blvd.,* ☎ *503/239–6087;* ✉ *2074 N.W. Lovejoy St.,* ☎ *503/227–4196.*

**\$** ✕ **Old Wives' Tales.** In this age when the religious right promulgates narrow notions of family values it's nice to find that one of the queerest restaurants in Portland has an extensively outfitted children's play area. This healthful, affordable, sunlit café draws plenty of dykes with tykes—and everybody else hankering for terrific Caesar salads, vegetarian burritos, fresh-baked goods, and other simple, wholesome fare. ⊠ *1300 E. Burnside St.,* ☎ *503/238–0470.*

**$** ✕ **Saigon Kitchen.** For the best spring roll in Portland head over the Broadway Bridge to this bustling Southeast Asian restaurant. The salted calamari, cashew chicken, and chili noodles with pork are big hits, and there's a long list of Thai stir-fry noodle dishes. The service is so quick it verges on being frantic. ⊠ *835 N.E. Broadway,* ☎ *503/281–3669.*

## Coffeehouse Culture

### West of the Willamette

**Coffee People.** There are a couple of Starbucks branches on Nob Hill, but the best spot for java is Coffee People, a tiny place with counter seating along the wall and front windows. They don't serve real food, but you can get great ice cream, shakes, and other sweets. ⊠ *533 N.W. 23rd Ave.,* ☎ *503/221–0235;* ⊠ *3500 S.E. Hawthorne Blvd.,* ☎ *503/235–1383.*

**Coffee Time.** With light-wood furniture, skylights, games and puzzles, and sidewalk seating below a few shade trees, Coffee Time has all the elements of a sunny- or rainy-day hangout. ⊠ *712 N.W. 21st Ave.,* ☎ *503/497–1090.*

### East of the Willamette

**Cafe Lena.** The brash and beatnik Cafe Lena has newspaper clippings and photos of Billie Holiday, Lenny Bruce, and other performers on the walls, disco music blaring when poetry readings aren't being staged, and great sandwiches (try the Birkenstock, a baguette with pesto mayo, veggies, and provolone). ⊠ *2239 S.E. Hawthorne Blvd.,* ☎ *503/238–7087.*

**Common Grounds.** An artsy but never fartsy bunch slips into this café by the Stark Raving Theatre for drop-dead-delicious shortbread cookies and invigorating caffeine brews. ⊠ *4321 S.E. Hawthorne Blvd.,* ☎ *503/236–4835.*

**Rimsky-Korsakoffee House.** This place has no sign out front and is staffed by smart-ass waitrons (the bad service is intentional—apparently somebody's idea of a marketing gimmick). The desserts are delicious, though, and folk musicians perform most nights. ⊠ *707 S.E. 12th Ave.,* ☎ *503/232–2640.*

**Utopia.** Here's one more gay-patronized spot for great coffee and desserts in the Hawthorne District. ⊠ *3220 S.E. Belmont St.,* ☎ *503/235–7606.*

# SCENES

Portland has a scruffy bar scene. You'll see plenty of beards and flannel shirts, hiking boots and Doc Martens, plus grungeware and even Deadhead chic. Visitors with fantasies about butch outdoorsy types and working-class heroes will find attractive pickings. (By the way, men who cut down trees in the forest are called loggers, *not* lumberjacks.) If you're even the least bit friendly, you'll have no trouble meeting people. There are dozens of bars, but this is not a major party town with pulsating warehouse discos and nonstop excitement. Queer locals complain that the nightlife crowd can be tired and insular, but outsiders will find enough to keep themselves amused for a few days.

Most places draw a decent mix of lesbians and gay men. The popular bars west of the Willamette are on Southwest Stark Street, and the hottest ones on the east side are on Southeast Stark Street. The several other options north of Burnside Street in the Old Town district are convivial neighborhood dives. Portland's taverns are open relatively late by West Coast standards, until 2:30 AM. They can't serve liquor unless they also serve food; many clubs either have (generally unexceptional) restaurants attached, or serve only beer and wine.

## West of the Willamette

PRIME SUSPECTS

**Boxx's/The Brig.** These two connected bars are gay Portland's favorite hangouts. What little stand-and-model action exists in the city you'll find here, though this is still a laid-back place. You enter through Boxx's, a nicely decorated, if typical, video bar with high cocktail tables and plenty of room for posing, mingling, and playing video poker. A hallway leads to the Brig, which has a pool table on one side and on the other a long bar overlooking a sunken dance floor. You can lean on the railings surrounding the small space and watch everybody wiggle, but the ambience is strangely grim, as though the designers had in mind the recreation room of a nuclear fallout shelter. The bartenders are sweet and friendly. ⊠ *1035 S.W. Stark St.,* ☎ *503/226–4171. Crowd: 75/25 m/f, mostly under 35, some guppies, clean-cut by Portland standards, cruisy.*

**City Nightclub.** One of the more recent—and much welcomed—additions to Portland nightlife is only open Friday and Saturday, but always draws a huge and varied crowd for dancing, drag shows, and the fag equivalent of American Bandstand (which is usually Friday). This large, impressive space in the heart of things gay has helped alleviate some of the tension in the neighborhood over the increasingly hetero crowds at Panorama (*see below*). ⊠ *13 N.W. 13th Ave.,* ☎ *503/224–2489. Crowd: 80/20 m/f, young (18 and older permitted), flashy, some stand-and-model.*

**Eagle.** Portland has a good leather scene, and the Eagle is where you'll find the most intense action. The first floor has a dark cruise bar, next to which is a smaller room with a pool table. Upstairs is an open interior balcony, a cozy aerie more conducive to conversation. In addition to the strong leather presence, you're apt to see some guys in creative uniforms—an Eagle Scout was spotted in here recently. ⊠ *1300 W. Burnside St.,* ☎ *503/241–0105. Crowd: male, mostly mid-20s to late 30s, mostly leather but some denim.*

**Embers.** This Old Town fixture was *the* hot disco for some time, but in the past couple of years it's begun to slide downhill, almost to the point of sliding back uphill in spite of itself (i.e., going retro). The main reason to come now is to catch one of the drag shows, held in the main disco. The front room is a dreary video lounge with a modestly campy appeal. ⊠ *110 N.W. Broadway,* ☎ *503/222–3082. Crowd: mostly gay but increasingly more straights, mixed m/f, all ages and races, loud and disorderly, some hustlers.*

**Hobo's.** Known more as a restaurant (*see* Eats, *above*), this huge steak house and lounge on the edge of Chinatown has piano music nightly. A large game room has pool tables, video games, and other diversions. ⊠ *120 N.W. 3rd Ave.,* ☎ *503/224–3285. Crowd: 80/20 gay/straight, mixed m/f, all ages.*

**Panorama.** It opened in 1994 with the aim of becoming Portland's first same-sex superclub, but despite being in the same overwhelmingly gay complex that houses Boxx's and the Brig, the crowd at Panorama has always been at least 50% hetero. It's a good place to dance, but tension between straights and gays pretty much kills the cruise factor. The crowd is unbelievably young—lots of rebellious kids from the burbs. On the plus side the decor is inventive and quirky, with a lively dance floor, one room with a bar and lounge chairs, and another done up in Moroccan-inspired furnishings, booth seating, and tall white columns. The club is open weekends until 4 AM. ⊠ *341 S.W. 10th Ave.,* ☎ *503/221–7262. Crowd: 50/50 gay/straight; mixed m/f; extremely young; serious dancers, poseurs; lots of spiked hair, shaved heads, body piercing.*

**Scandals.** This is the mellowest of Southwest Stark Street's several bars, a casual beer-and-wine tavern with big windows looking onto the street. There's a long bar, video games, and plenty of diversions inside; many people here seem to know one another. Great drink specials on Tuesday nights help pump up the crowds. On weekends, an adjacent espresso bar and gallery is open. ⊠ *1038 S.W. Stark St.,* ☎ *503/227–5887. Crowd: mostly male, blue-collar, over 35, regular guys, local, very friendly.*

**Silverado.** Were it not in the heart of the gay entertainment section, this would be just another hustler bar with strippers. Instead, it's all that and so much more. You enter an oddly configured room with a long bar up front. Across from that is a small stage for the (mostly) gangly strippers, with a counter and seats around it on which patrons can rest their asses and their highballs yet still be close enough to stick dollar bills in as many waistbands as possible. A DJ spins mostly dated disco for the small dance floor in the far corner. The lighting here has a florid pink tint that makes everybody's denim appear acid-washed—or maybe it's just that everybody's denim *is* acid-washed. Off the main bar a small dining room has booths and a ship's wheel on the wall. ⊠ *1217 S.W. Stark St.,* ☎ *503/224–4493. Crowd: mostly male, chickens and chickenhawks, racially mixed, a few drag queens, hard drinkers, rough-and-ready, overall sleazy but kind of fun.*

### NEIGHBORHOOD HAUNTS

**C. C. Slaughter's** (⊠ 1014 S.W. Stark St., ☎ 503/248–9135), Portland's country-western dance hall, is mostly male and similar to its counterparts in other cities. **Darcelle XV** (⊠ 208 N.W. 3rd Ave., ☎ 503/222–5338) is famous among gays and straights for its elaborate drag revues; on nights the gals don't dress up, strippers dress down. Leather bears head to the **Dirty Duck** (⊠ 439 N.W. 3rd Ave., ☎ 503/224–8446), a dirty old pub in an industrial area. The **Fox and Hound** (⊠ 217 N.W. 2nd Ave., ☎ 503/243–5530) in the Old Town district serves up sandwiches and burgers, karaoke, and a saucy crowd of locals. **Ray's Ordinary** (⊠ 317 N.W. Broadway, ☎ 503/222–7297), another gritty Old Town spot, has live piano music some nights.

# East of the Willamette

### PRIME SUSPECTS

**Choices.** Though predominantly lesbian, this chummy pub east of the river welcomes most everyone. The large brightly lit place has two pool tables, a rockin' jukebox, a small dance floor, darts, and a couple of large-screen TVs. Very outgoing staff. ⊠ *2845 S.E. Stark St.,* ☎ *503/236–4321. Crowd: mostly gay, 80/20 f/m, all ages, all types.*

**Joq's.** Once a simple blue-collar drinking hole, Joq's attracts more diverse patrons these days. Still basically a place where locals dish and rub elbows, it now gets crowded early most evenings; weekends can get downright packed. The bar is filled with the usual amusements: pool, videos, and lottery machines. Extremely friendly bartenders. ⊠ *2512 N.E. Broadway,* ☎ *503/287–4210. Crowd: mostly male, all ages, steady mix of regulars and newcomers, zero attitude.*

### NEIGHBORHOOD HAUNTS

**Starky's** (⊠ 2913 S.E. Stark St., ☎ 503/230–7980), a warm, terrific lounge in eastern Portland, has a restaurant that serves the usual pub fare. Men and women are welcome.

# Hangin' with the Hets

In addition to the specifically queer clubs listed above, **La Luna** (⊠ 215 S.E. 9th Ave., ☎ 503/241–5862) has long been a Portland institution for cutting-edge music and alternative performances. A young crowd of gays and straights filters in here just about every night of the week. Mondays ($5 cover) are queer nights. The **Candlelight Room** (⊠ 2032 S.W. 5th Ave., ☎ 503/222–3378) by Portland State University is a dark, smoky, gay-friendly place with pool tables and live alternative music.

**Bar of the Gods** (⊠ 4801 S.E. Hawthorne Blvd., ☎ 503/226–4171) and **Squeeze Box** (⊠ Sauce Box Restaurant, 214 S.W. Broadway, ☎ 503/241–3393) are two trendoid lounges that draw a steady stream of grungers, hipsters, and homos.

# Beyond Portland

## Vancouver, Washington

Close enough to be considered a suburb of Portland, the town of Vancouver, Washington, has a significant lesbian and gay

community and a popular hangout, the **North Bank Tavern**
(⊠ 106 W. 6th St., ☎ 360/695–3862).

## Salem

The state capital has a wildly fun neighborhood dance bar,
**Sneakers** (⊠ 300 Liberty St. SE, ☎ 503/363–0549), which
draws a true mix of characters, from alternateens to older
couples out to shake their booties. Not as many dykes and
straights come here, but all are welcome. The dance floor is
substantial, the music eclectic, and the bar's dusty-rose walls,
natural-wood furniture, and large windows overlooking a
park are a welcome alternative to the dreary atmosphere of
some nightclubs. The trendy restaurant here serves regional
American food.

# Action

Washington Park is called the Fruit Loop. As you approach
the park from the city, the loop, to which there is no auto
access at night, is across from the reservoir.

There are a few adult bookshops, but both **Fantasy Video**
(⊠ 3137 N.E. Sandy Blvd., ☎ 503/239–6969; ⊠ 1512 W.
Burnside St., ☎ 503/244–6969) stores are open 24 hours,
are cruisy, and have busy video arcades. There's a bathhouse, **Club Portland** (⊠ 303 S.W. 12th Ave., ☎ 503/227–
9992), in the heart of the downtown bar strip.

## Gay Beaches

**Rooster Rock State Park** (☎ 503/695–2261), a.k.a. Cock
Rock, lies 20 miles east of the city on U.S. 84 in scenic
Columbia Gorge. Nearby mountain ranges form the backdrop.
Nudity is permitted at the beach; The gay section is to the right,
along the river, about a half mile up. The nude beach at
**Sauvies Island** is about 8 miles northwest of Portland on U.S.
30. After taking the bridge to Sauvies Island, turn right onto
N.W. Gillihan Loop Road and follow this for some time before making a right onto N.W. Reeder Road. Parking for the
gay section is near the end of Reeder Road in the last lot. When
you reach the banks of the Columbia River, turn left and walk
about 10 or 15 minutes until you start noticing the throngs
of queers—the numbers can be very high on sunny weekends.
These two beaches go back and forth in popularity, but
Rooster Rock definitely has the cruisiest reputation.

# SLEEPS

Portland has several outstanding European-style hotels, most in century-old buildings and all within a short walk of the Pearl District's gay bars. Several are high-end, but three excellent ones charge as little as $60 nightly. All the major chain hotels are represented in Portland.

For price ranges, *see* Chart B at the front of this guide.

## Hotels

**$$$–**
**$$$$** ☷ **Benson Hotel.** The lobby of Portland's 1912 grande dame is simply stunning. Guest rooms are less fancy but perfectly charming, with many original architectural details and such touches as crystal chandeliers. ⊠ *309 S. W. Broadway, 97205,* ☎ *503/228–2000 or 800/426–0670,* ℻ *503/226–4603. 287 rooms. Restaurant, exercise room.*

**$$$–**
**$$$$** ☷ **Fifth Avenue Suites.** This new Kimpton Group addition to downtown borrows a familiar Portland strategy: Take a classy old building (in this case a 1912 structure that most recently housed the Frederick & Nelson Department Store) and convert it into a charming hotel. The twist here is that each of the richly decorated rooms is a full suite with a spacious sitting area. The concierge and staff are top-notch and can direct you to great restaurants and fun bars. A first-rate property all around. ⊠ *506 S. W. Washington St., 97205,* ☎ *503/222–0001 or 800/711–2971,* ℻ *503/222–0004. 221 rooms. Restaurant, exercise room.*

**$$$–**
**$$$$** ☷ **Governor Hotel.** Before the 1909 Governor Building was converted into this posh hotel, its gutted interior starred as the home of a raffish posse of ne'er-do-wells and their Faginesque leader in Gus Van Sant's film *My Own Private Idaho.* They wouldn't recognize it now: Murals in the lobby depict scenes from Lewis and Clark's Columbia River expedition, public rooms have dark mahogany detailing and a lodgelike rusticity, and the guest rooms are sumptuous and softly lit. The restaurant, Jake's Grill, serves highly regarded American cuisine. ⊠ *6119 S. W. 10th St., 97205,* ☎ *503/224–3400 or 800/554–3456,* ℻ *503/241–2122. 100 rooms. Restaurant, pool, exercise room.*

**$$$–**
**$$$$** ☷ **Hotel Vintage Plaza.** A fully restored historic downtown building holds one of the spiffiest properties in the Pacific Northwest. The rooms are large and done in warm colors;

17 have hot tubs, and some of the suites have spiral staircases leading to second-story sleeping lofts. A complimentary wine reception takes place evenings in the lobby. The on-site Pazzo is one of the better Italian restaurants downtown. ✉ *422 S.W. Broadway, 97205,* ☎ *503/228–1212 or 800/243–0555,* ℻ *503/228–3598. 107 rooms. Restaurant, exercise room.*

$–$$ 🏨 **Imperial Hotel.** This full-of-character 1908 hotel is as good a budget option as you'll find in any major city. It looks and feels nearly as nice as its luxury-hotel neighbors, and though it lacks some of their business services and amenities, it's nevertheless a classy property with good-size rooms. ✉ *400 S.E. Broadway, 97205,* ☎ *503/228–7221 or 800/452–2323,* ℻ *503/223–4551. 136 rooms. Restaurant.*

$–$$ 🏨 **Mallory Hotel.** The same folks who run the Imperial also operate this classic (1920s), dependable, affordable choice just a 10-minute walk from the gay bars on Stark Street. Rooms here are similarly clean and cheerful. Book well in advance spring through early fall. ✉ *729 S.W. 15th St., 97205,* ☎ *503/223–6311 or 800/228–8657,* ℻ *503/223–0522. 144 rooms. Restaurant.*

$ 🏨 **Mark Spencer Hotel.** Steps from the gay bars, the Mark Spencer looks unsavory from the outside but is clean and comfortable inside. Basic and dirt cheap (weekly rates are especially good), its rooms come with walk-in closets and kitchens. Rates include a complimentary Continental breakfast. ✉ *409 S.W. 11th Ave., 97205,* ☎ *503/224–3293 or 800/548–3934,* ℻ *503/223–7848. 101 rooms.*

$ 🏨 **Motel 6.** This no-frills chain property in southeast Portland puts you close to the Hawthorne District. ✉ *3104 S.E. Powell Blvd., 97214,* ☎ *503/238–0600 or 800/466–8358,* ℻ *503/238–7167. 69 rooms.*

## Guest Houses and Small Hotels

$–$$ 🏨 **MacMaster House.** On swank King's Hill, which looms above downtown, and just two blocks from Washington Park, this grand turn-of-the-century Colonial Revival home is convenient to the business district. The rooms have a romantic mix of antiques and reproductions, and four have fireplaces. Complimentary wine is served in the afternoon. The gourmet breakfasts here are highly acclaimed. ✉ *1041 S.W. Vista Ave., 97205,* ☎ *503/223–7362 or 800/774–9523,* ℻

*503/224–8808. 7 rooms, 2 with phone, 2 with private bath, all with TV. Full breakfast. Mixed gay/straight.*

**$   ▥ Holladay House B&B.** This 1922 Dutch Colonial in northeast Portland is a short walk from ʳhe Lloyd Center mall and also quite close to the burgeoning gay shopping and dining scene on Broadway. Rooms are homey and casual, with a few antiques. ⊠ *1735 N.E. Wasco St., 97232,* ☎ *503/282–3172. 2 rooms share a bath. Full breakfast. Mostly straight.*

**$   ▥ Sullivan's Gulch B&B.** The gay-operated Sullivan's Gulch is in a modest residential neighborhood across the Willamette, close to the emerging Northeast Broadway gay business district. Rooms in the art-filled, 1904 Colonial Revival home are comfortably furnished with Western and Native American art; a deck in back overlooks well-tended gardens. Hosts Skip and Jack are friendly and knowledgeable. ⊠ *1744 N.E. Clackamas St., 97232,* ☎ *503/331–1104. 3 rooms, 2 with private bath, all with TV. Continental breakfast. Mixed gay male, lesbian, straight.*

# THE LITTLE BLACK BOOK

## At Your Fingertips

**Cascade AIDS Project** (☎ 503/223–6339, ext. 111). **Lesbian Community Project** (☎ 503/223–0071). **Lesbian Health Project** (☎ 503/236–8770). **Gay and Lesbian Archives for the Pacific Northwest** (☎ 503/284–1872). **Gay Resource Connection** (☎ 503/223–2437 or 800/777–2437). **Oregon AIDS Hotline** (☎ 503/223–2437 or 800/777–2437). **Phoenix Rising** (☎ 503/223–8299; queer youth support). **Portland Oregon Visitors Association** (⊠ 3 World Trade Center, 97204, ☎ 503/275–9750; events hot line, ☎ 503/222–2223).

## Gay Media

*Just Out* (☎ 503/236–1252) is the biweekly gay and lesbian newspaper. Just across the Columbia River from Portland, the small city of Vancouver, Washington, has a monthly gay and lesbian newspaper, the *Vancouver Voice* (☎ 360/737–9879).

Portland's several progressive arts and entertainment papers include *PDXS* (☎ 503/224–7316) and the *Rocket* (☎ 503/228–4702). Both are biweekly and focus on the local music scene. The more comprehensive *Willamette Week* (☎ 503/243–2122) is extremely pro-gay.

BOOKSTORES

**Gai-Pied** (✉ 2544 N.E. Broadway, ☎ 503/331–1125), pronounced gay *pee* ay, opened recently in the Northeast Broadway district. The gay-male bookstore began in a small space with a selection of books, magazines, and videos, and has already expanded; it now also carries novelties, and there are plans to add a café. **Twenty-Third Avenue Books** (✉ 1015 N.W. 23rd Ave., ☎ 503/224–5097) has an excellent selection of lesbian and gay titles; it was Portland's unofficial queer bookstore until Gai-Pied opened. **In Other Words** (✉ 3734 S.E. Hawthorne Blvd., ☎ 503/232–6003) carries feminist and lesbian books and videos, plus many children's titles. This is a great place for lesbians to find resources and social opportunities. **It's My Pleasure** (✉ 4258 S.E. Hawthorne Blvd., ☎ 503/236–0505) is a fun lesbian-oriented sex boutique with books, magazines, and movies. **The Crimson Phoenix** (✉ 1876 S.W. 5th Ave., ☎ 503/228–0129) dedicates itself to all forms of human sexuality; it has many titles about lesbian and gay sex. The enormous **Powell's City of Books** (✉ 1005 W. Burnside St., ☎ 503/228–4651) has an amazing selection of used titles, including lesbian and gay ones.

## Working Out

The well-appointed **YWCA** (✉ 1111 S.W. 10th Ave., ☎ 503/294–7440) gym and swim center is extremely dyke-positive. Downtown gay men and lesbians favor the fancy **Princeton (a.k.a. "Princess") Athletic Club** (✉ 614 S.W. 11th Ave., ☎ 503/222–2639). The downtown **Gold's Gym** (✉ 1210 N.W. Johnson St., ☎ 503/222–1210) is favored by gays and straights, as is the **Gold's Gym** (✉ 4121 N.E. Halsey St., ☎ 503/281–4767) in the Hollywood District.

# 6 *Out in Eugene*

**E**UGENE IS OREGON'S THROWBACK to '60s activism. Eugene Skinner founded this upbeat university town at the southern end of the Willamette Valley in 1846. It prospered for the next century as a shipping and trading hub, and developed an intense counterculture during the 1960s. The city is often named in polls as one of America's most livable communities, which to cynics means, "Oh, nice place to live but who'd want to visit?" To be sure, this is not a tourist mecca, but it is a vibrant center for education, the arts, and outdoor activities—there's plenty here to keep you busy for a few days.

As for the lesbian and gay community, it has the resources and networking of a place five times Eugene's size, with successful fund-raising and community service groups, women's social and professional organizations, and a thriving Metropolitan Community Church. The Eugene Human Rights Commission, formed more than three decades ago, monitors acts of discrimination and conducts sensitivity trainings. The lesbian, gay, and bisexual alliance at the University of Oregon (U. of O.) is one of the oldest continuously running such groups in the country. It's no surprise, then, that U. of O. has one of the most hate-free campuses you'll ever find.

Not that all is rosy. Neighboring Springfield hatched Oregon's well-publicized antigay ballot initiatives. For much of the 1990s Eugene and other queer-friendly locales have fought hard across the state to buck a homophobic tide. Their efforts have largely paid off (though the antigay contingent in the Willamette Valley remains active), and the experience has drawn the community together and heightened the awareness of gay issues among many straights.

But don't let this talk of polarization scare you off: The majority of Eugene's residents are progressive, open, and tolerant. A recent transplant says that life in this mellow city has vastly rearranged her priorities, that she's much better able now to stop and appreciate both her surroundings and the people around her. Another local jokes that there is Pacific Standard Time, and then there is Eugene time; if you set your mental watch to the latter, you won't get anything done in a hurry but you won't mind either. You hear good things about this town wherever you go—expect a warm welcome and a laid-back good time.

# THE LAY OF THE LAND

Eugene is at the southern end of the Willamette River Valley; two major rivers join with the Willamette near town, the McKenzie (just north of it) and the Middle Fork (to the south). I–5 divides what is essentially a twin-city region, with Eugene to the west and Springfield to the east. Hills surround the city, and in general the area is wooded, green, and sprinkled with parks.

## Downtown

The Willamette River curves in a southeasterly direction through Eugene, fringed with bike trails and walkways and traversed by a couple of pedestrian bridges. The river had industrial uses during the 19th century, but today it's mostly the domain of picnickers, strollers, sun bunnies, and cyclists. Attractions include the **Owen Rose Garden** (⊠ Jefferson St., north end, ☎ 541/687–5220), where more than 4,500 varieties grow. East of here you can climb to the butte that gives **Skinner Butte Park** its name for amazing views of town. There are trailhead signs along Skinner Butte Loop, at the base of the hill. Immense Victorians homes dot the streets below the hill, material proof of Eugene's success as a river port.

For the most part, downtown Eugene is a pleasure to walk. The one exception is a bungled late-1960s attempt at urban renewal in the dozen or so blocks around Willamette Street and 12th Avenue, where late-19th- and early-20th-century structures were razed and replaced with characterless buildings. The city center is on the mend, however, and some fun shops have opened in recent years.

A former chicken-processing plant houses the gay-popular **Fifth Street Public Market** (⊠ 5th Ave. and High St., ☎ 541/484–0383). The complex has fascinating shops and enticing ethnic and conventional restaurants. Be sure to sample the fresh and delicious food (and sweet green tea) at the **Metropol Bakery** (☎ 541/687–9370). For new threads, lesbians love **Folkways Imports** (☎ 541/343–8667). Gay men frequently browse the racks at **Global Traveler** (☎ 541/683–1124).

From April through December, locals descend upon the nearby **Saturday Market** (⊠ 8th Ave., between Willamette and Pearl Sts., ☎ 541/686–8885), where entertainers perform and close to 200 artisans, farmers, and cooks sell their wares.

Eugene has an extensive arts scene for a city its size. Much of the cultural activity revolves around the **Hult Center for the Performing Arts** (⊠ 7th Ave. and Willamette St., ☎ 541/687–5000), one of the most impressive facilities of its type in the Pacific Northwest. The 1982 building houses a theater and concert hall, where the city's fine ballet, opera, and symphony perform regularly.

Exhibits and artifacts of southern Oregon's industrial and logging history fill the **Lane County Historical Museum** (⊠ 740 W. 13th Ave., ☎ 541/687–4239) west of downtown.

Across the Willamette north of downtown is **Valley River Center** (⊠ 293 Valley River Center, ☎ 541/683–5511), the largest such complex between San Francisco and Portland. Just because you're in eco-conscious healthnik land doesn't mean you can't find a thriving enclosed-mall culture, complete with bratty mall rats. The food court here is pretty decent, too.

## The University of Oregon

Walk several blocks east of downtown to reach the leafy, eminently strollable campus of the **University of Oregon** (☎ 541/346–3014 or 541/346–3009), most easily accessed from 13th Avenue. The **University of Oregon Museum of Art** (☎ 541/346–3027) near the corner of 13th Avenue and Kincaid Street has a permanent collection strong on works from China, Japan, Korea, Cambodia, Russia, and Africa. Regional photography and art are well represented. Also worth visiting is the **Museum of Natural History–University of Oregon** (⊠ 1680 E. 15th Ave., ☎ 541/346–3024). The university's main commercial drag, **13th Avenue,** is loaded with cheap restaurants and engaging shops.

North of campus across Franklin Boulevard the Autzen Foot Bridge leads across the Willamette River into **Alton Baker Park,** which is ideal for biking and hiking. You can return by way of the Knickerbocker Bike Bridge, at the park's east end. Also near campus, you can hike among 300-year-old Douglas firs in 47-acre **Hendricks Park** (⊠ Heights Blvd., reached via Franklin Blvd. and then Agate St., ☎ 541/687–5220), which runs along southeastern Eugene's wooded ridge. The gardens here hold flora from around the world plus 10 acres of rhododendrons and azaleas that are spectacular when in bloom.

## South of Downtown

Willamette Street south through downtown leads to 2,065-foot **Spencer Butte.** Several trailheads wind to the peak; the Ridgeline Trail is a bit strenuous but passes through colorful blooming bushes and stands of Douglas fir. On your way to the park slow down around the 2400 block of Willamette Street—there are several crunchy shops, natural food markets (good for picnic supplies), and inexpensive restaurants.

Southeast of town (take I–5 to the 30th Avenue exit) lies **Mt. Pisgah Arboretum** (⊠ 34909 Frank Parrish Rd., ☎ 541/747–3817), a 120-acre plant sanctuary with trails, wildflower meadows, and a conifer forest.

## Springfield

Everything that Eugene is—progressive, erudite, outgoing—its sister-city Springfield is not. Gays and lesbians should be cautious wandering through this conservative suburb. The one bright note is the historic downtown district, along Franklin Boulevard, which has galleries, antiques shops, and a historical interpretive center.

## The McKenzie River Valley

Eugene is in the center of Lane County. A popular day trip takes in **Highway 126** alongside the **McKenzie River,** which flows east of Eugene for about 50 miles to the bucolic village of **McKenzie Bridge.** From here, between May and October, you can drive another 35 twisting miles along **Highway 242** to 5,325-foot **McKenzie Pass.** In winter McKenzie Pass road is closed, and even in good weather you should proceed only if you are prepared for some truly scary hairpin curves and steep inclines.

Highway 126 passes by countless waterfalls and has views of the **Cascades** and **Three Sisters** mountain ranges. Highway 242 winds through barren, moonlike lava fields. For information on the region, contact the **McKenzie River Chamber of Commerce** (⊠ Box 1117, Leaburg 97489, ☎ 541/896–3330). For advice on hiking, camping, and cycling, the **McKenzie River Ranger Station** (⊠ 57600 Hwy. 126, McKenzie Bridge 97413, ☎ 541/822–3381).

## Corvallis

Corvallis, 43 miles north of Eugene in the heart of the Willamette River Valley, is laced with scenic drives, wineries, covered bridges, recreational areas, and several museums. The **Benton County Historical Museum** (⊠ 1101 Main St., ☎ 541/929–6230) gives an excellent overview of the region's history. Downtown Corvallis, home to **Oregon State University** (OSU), is filled with cheap cafés and offbeat shops, including a homo-popular bookstore, **Grass Roots** (⊠ 227 S.W. 2nd St., ☎ 541/754–7668); attached is a café and espresso bar that draws boho types, artsy students, and cute young things. Mary's Peak, 16 miles west of Corvallis, the highest of the Coast Range Mountains, is ideal for hiking in warm weather and cross-country skiing in winter.

Corvallis may not be quite as countercultural or as big a city as Eugene, but there is a visible queer presence (though if you ask about nightlife you'll be greeted with shrugs and chuckles). OSU has a **Lesbian, Gay, and Bisexual Alliance** (⊠ 249 Snell St., MU East, ☎ 541/737–6360). **After 8** (☎ 541/752–8157) is another resource; it's a lesbigay referral and social group that can offer newcomers and visitors advice about where to go and what to do. You'll probably have to leave a message on their voice mail, but somebody will usually check back with you soon after.

# GETTING AROUND

Eugene is a couple of hours south of Portland via I–5, and a couple of hours north of Ashland and Medford (down near the California border). As I–5 slices between Eugene and Springfield, I–105 breaks off to the west into downtown Eugene. Greyhound and Amtrak come into Eugene, which also has a municipal airport that's served by Horizon, American, Alaska, and United airlines.

You can walk around downtown, the U. of O. campus, and the points in between. The sights farther afield require a car, but this is excellent biking territory—if you're only going as far as one of the parks on the outskirts of town, consider cycling. The city has an extensive bus system, but short-term visitors won't find much reason to use it.

# WHEN TO GO

Late June is a great time to come to Eugene, for the splendid weather and the **Oregon Bach Festival** (☎ 541/346–5666 or 800/457–1486), which showcases classical and jazz music. During this time, usually around the last weekend in June, Eugene celebrates its **gay pride day** (☎ 541/346–3360). Two weeks later granola queens won't want to miss heading 20 minutes west of downtown to the **Oregon Country Faire** (☎ 541/343–4298). You can pick up herbs, incense, Grateful Dead bootlegs, crafts, and every other vestige of hippiedom. It's a great deal of fun.

# EATS

In a town with a strong left-political identity it's not surprising that restaurants brag of their organic ingredients, multi-ethnic menus, and ambitious recycling programs. Fortunately, this is not all a gimmick. The food here is good, and the prices reasonable. Just about every place is queer-friendly, and the gay Club Arena (*see* Scenes, *below*) has a restaurant (Pass the Pepper) with decent American fare.

Natural-foods groceries and bakeries are a way of life in Eugene. Most have dining areas where it's easy to meet new friends. The **L & L Market** is reviewed below, but also consider **Friendly Foods & Deli** (⊠ 2757 Friendly St., ☎ 541/683–2079), **The Kiva** (⊠ 125 W. 11th Ave., ☎ 541/342–8666), **Oasis Fine Foods Marketplace** (⊠ 2489 Willamette St., ☎ 541/345–1014; ⊠ Coburg Rd., off Willakenzie Rd., ☎ 541/334–6382), and the **Palace Bakery** (⊠ 45 E. 8th Ave., ☎ 541/484–2435).

$$$ ✕ **La Chanterelle.** Fresh flowers and fine china set the tone for a romantic evening in this slightly formal restaurant where you needn't be dressed to the nines. Classic French cui-

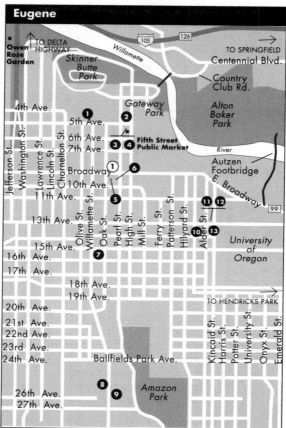

# Eugene

**Eats** ●

Ambrosia, **5**

Cafe
Navarro, **1**

Cafe Zenon, **6**

Caspian
Mediterranean
Cafe, **11**

Coffee
Corner, **4**

Coffee
People, **13**

Espresso
Roma, **12**

Glenwood
Cafe, **8, 10**

L & L
Market, **7**

La
Chanterelle, **2**

Mekala's, **3**

Santa Fe
Burrito
Company, **9**

**Scenes** ○

Club Arena/
Pass the
Pepper, **1**

sine is subtly seasoned and skillfully presented. ⊠ *207 E. 5th Ave.,* ☎ *541/484–4065.*

**$$–$$$** ✕ **Ambrosia.** This lively spot close to downtown and the U. of O. serves creative wood-fired pizzas, delicious pasta dishes, and savory northern Italian seafood and meat grills that employ regional ingredients. Many folks stop by the bar to sample hard-to-find Italian vintages. ⊠ *174 E. Broadway Ave.,* ☎ *541/342–4141.*

**$$–$$$** ✕ **Cafe Zenon.** If the Zenon were a house of worship, it would be named the Church of the Reformed Hippie. Former draft dodgers and bra burners descend upon this chic little café for spirited world-beat food, including beef in a hot Indian curry, grilled quail, and numerous veggie dishes. Old-fashioned street lamps, marble tables, and slate floors lend a festive air. ⊠ *898 Pearl St.,* ☎ *541/343–3005.*

**$$** ✕ **Cafe Navarro.** Since it opened a few years ago everybody in Eugene has been raving about this pan-ethnic eatery that specializes in spicy Latin American, Caribbean, and African fare. Tropical colors and vibrant music add to the fun and keep the steady stream of gays and straights happy. ⊠ *454 Willamette St.,* ☎ *541/344–0943.*

**$–$$** ✕ **Mekala's.** Signature dishes at what is arguably the finest of the Fifth Street Public Market restaurants include the chicken with cashew nuts, celery, and onions; pineapple with carrots, peas, lime leaves, tofu, and bamboo shoots in a red curry sauce; and a snapper stir-fried with fresh sliced ginger, mushrooms, onions, and red wine. ⊠ *296 E. 5th Ave.,* ☎ *541/342–4872.*

**$** ✕ **Caspian Mediterranean Cafe.** This student-infested café with a glorified fast-food ambience serves great cheap chow: wood-fired pizzas, spinach curry, mint-yogurt dip, and many other Middle Eastern specials. The dining room is modest, but there's seating out on a patio with antique iron furniture. ⊠ *863 E. 13th Ave.,* ☎ *541/683–7800.*

**$** ✕ **Glenwood Cafe.** There are two branches of this homo-popular eatery in town; the south side location is a little bigger and brighter than the one near campus, a major student haunt where the queer youth groups often hang before or after meetings. Breakfast at both places is a specialty, but at all meals you'll find better-than-average diner favorites, such as pastas, sandwiches, and several egg scrambles. ⊠ *1340 Alder St.,* ☎ *541/687–0355;* ⊠ *2588 Willamette St.,* ☎ *541/687–8201.*

$  ✕ **L & L Market.** A complex of several great shops is the ultimate stopover for delicious food and low-key lesbian cruising. The highlight (at least of the shops) is the French Horn bakery, which has outstanding pastries, sandwiches, and salads. The L&L also holds a coffeehouse, a deli, a wine shop, and a bookstore. An enormous seating area in the center of the market hops with chatty locals. ⊠ *1591 Willamette St.,* ☎ *541/686–2985.*

$  ✕ **Santa Fe Burrito Company.** It may not be much fancier than a Taco Bell, but this purveyor of short-order southwestern food has the best burritos (most of them under $3) in town. The spicy pork verde and bean burrito is one favorite; also good are the cheese, black bean, and chicken quesadillas. ⊠ *2621 Willamette St.,* ☎ *541/465–1113. No credit cards.*

## Coffeehouse Culture

Eugene has several fairly homo- and student-popular coffeehouses. **Coffee Corner** (⊠ 296 E. 5th Ave., ☎ 541/343–7230) has space for espresso sipping on two floors. Near the University, check out snazzy, mod (the furniture includes some cool chairs fashioned to resemble exotic drums) **Coffee People** (⊠ 840 E. 13th Ave., ☎ 541/302–1771). Bright but spare **Espresso Roma** (⊠ 825 E. 13th Ave., ☎ 541/484–0878) across the street draws an artsy crowd.

# SCENES

With but one queer bar Eugene is hardly a major party center. If you're visiting while school is in session (September through June), it's worth calling the U. of O.'s gay, lesbian, and bisexual alliance (☎ 541/346–3360) about parties or social events. Many are open to the public.

**Club Arena/Pass the Pepper** (⊠ 959 Pearl St., ☎ 541/683–2360) is the local gay entertainment complex. The upstairs Pass the Pepper, a lounge-restaurant (traditional American food), has darts, pool, video screens, and room for mingling. Downstairs at Club Arena all ages, genders, and types, including hip hets, gather for disco frivolity. Sunday '70s and '80s dance parties are plenty of fun. Outsiders will have little trouble making friends. Unfortunately there's no place here for the under-21 set.

### Action

The area's one shop for queer erotica, lingerie, and toys is, oddly, in conservative Springfield. **Exclusively Adult** (✉ 1166 South A St., ☎ 541/726–6969) is open nearly 24 hours daily and has all your favorite vids and mags. There are no sex clubs or even particularly cruisy parks in the region.

# SLEEPS

Eugene has a handful of historic bed-and-breakfast inns, many student-oriented budget motels, and a few business hotels, but it's not known for the character or variety of its accommodations.

$$–$$$ 🏨 **Eugene Hilton.** The luxury business hotel in town, adjacent to the convention center and Hult Center, is not all that fancy. Rooms have pleasant but nondescript chain furnishings. ✉ 66 E. 6th Ave., 97401, ☎ 541/342–2000 or 800/445–8667, FAX 541/342–6661. 270 rooms. 2 restaurants, pool, exercise room.

$$ 🏨 **Best Western New Oregon.** Directly across from campus and a short walk from the pedestrian bridge to Alton Baker Park, this smart chain motel has extensive facilities considering the rates. ✉ 1655 Franklin Blvd., 97401, ☎ 541/683–3669 or 800/528–1234, FAX 541/484–5556. 129 rooms. Pool.

$ 🏨 **66 Motel.** A popular choice of budget-minded students, the 66 has simple, clean rooms. Rates are dirt-cheap, and campus is just a short walk south. You won't go wrong here if luxury is not a requirement. ✉ 755 E. Broadway Ave., 97401, ☎ 541/342–5041. 66 rooms.

## Guest Houses and Small Hotels

$$–$$$ 🏨 **Excelsior Inn.** Adjacent to the U. of O. campus and until recently a housing unit for female students, the Excelsior was transformed into one of Oregon's finest small hotels. Rooms, named for classical composers, range from cozy doubles with hardwood floors and arched windows to full suites with marble baths, VCRs, and vaulted ceilings. Breakfast downstairs in the excellent Excelsior Cafe is a treat. The restaurant is also popular for lunch and dinner. ✉ 754 E. 13th Ave., 97401, ☎ 541/342–1417 or 800/321–6963, FAX 541/342–

*1417. 14 rooms with phone, TV, and private bath. Full breakfast. Mostly straight.*

**$$** 🏨 **Campbell House Inn.** This handsome Queen Anne in Eugene's downtown historic district is two blocks from riverfront bike paths. Some rooms have fireplaces, and all have Waverly print fabrics, brass beds, cherry-wood furniture, and access to an acre of gardens. ⊠ *252 Pearl St., 97401,* ☎ *541/343–1119 or 800/264–2519,* FAX *541/343–2258. 14 rooms, with phone, TV, and private bath. Full breakfast. Mostly straight.*

---

# THE LITTLE BLACK BOOK

## At Your Fingertips

**All Women's Health Services** (☎ 541/342–5940). **Corvallis Convention and Visitors Bureau** (⊠ 420 N.W. 2nd St., ☎ 541/757–1544 or 800/334–8118). **Eugene Convention and Visitors Association** (⊠ 115 W. 8th Ave., Suite 190, Box 10286, 97401, ☎ 541/484–5307 or 800/547–5445). **Gay and Lesbian Alliance** (☎ 541/672–4126). **HIV Alliance** (☎ 541/342–5088). **Springfield Area Chamber of Commerce** (⊠ 101 South A St., Box 155, 97477, ☎ 541/746–1651). **University of Oregon Lesbian, Gay, and Bisexual Alliance** (⊠ Suite 319, EMU, U. of O. campus, ☎ 541/346–3360). **Valley AIDS Information Network** (☎ 541/752–6322 or 800/588–AIDS). **Womenspace Lesbian Alliance Hotline** (☎ 541/485–6513 or 800/281–2800).

## Gay Media

The monthly *View Magazine* (☎ 541/302–6523) is Oregon's main lesbian and gay newspaper, but it's based in Eugene, so the city coverage is good. The well-written paper is strong on op-ed pieces and local political coverage. *Connections* (☎ 541/485–0890) is the region's lesbigay business directory.

The free arts- and entertainment-oriented *Eugene Weekly* (☎ 541/484–0519) carries lesbian and gay community stories and listings. Also worth a look is the bimonthly *Elixir* (☎ 541/710–0553), a spunky 'zine covering hip music and cutting-edge style that doesn't overlook the queer scene. It's free in Eugene, and $3 elsewhere.

### BOOKSTORES

For women's books, cards, music, and community resources try **Mother Kali's Books** (⊠ 720 E. 13th Ave., ☎ 541/343–

4864) near the U. of O. campus. Specializing in New Age, holistic, spiritual, and progressive books is **Peralandra** (⊠ Station Square, 199 E. 5th Ave., ☎ 541/485–4848), across from the Fifth Street Public Market. If you still haven't found just the right book to curl up with, comb through the racks at the **University of Oregon Bookstore** (⊠ E. 13th Ave. and Kincaid St., ☎ 541/346–4331), which has just about everything.

## Working Out

It's fun to play at the **YMCA** (⊠ 2055 Patterson St., ☎ 541/686–9622).

# 7 Elsewhere in the Pacific Northwest

## ASHLAND, OREGON

**F**ROM FEBRUARY THROUGH LATE OCTOBER, Ashland, which is just north of the California border, is home to the prestigious **Oregon Shakespeare Festival** (✉ 15 S. Pioneer St., Ashland, OR 97520, ☎ 541/482–4331). The Ashland region's myriad outdoor diversions range from hiking to skiing. New Agers, feminists, and gays have long been fixtures here—you'll find the area extremely tolerant. **Bloomsbury Books** (✉ 290 E. Main St., ☎ 541/488–0029), a mainstream independent, has a solid lesbigay section. For price ranges, *see* Chart B at the front of this guide.

### Eats and Scenes

Ashland is a great town for eating out, with relatively affordable queer-popular options. The owners of San Francisco's Flying Saucer restaurant operate the **Firefly Restaurant** (✉ 15 N. 1st St., ☎ 541/488–3212; $$–$$$), where inventive New American cuisine is the rule. For contemporary French cuisine, including many salads, try **Monet** (✉ 36 S. 2nd St., ☎ 541/482–1339; $$–$$$), which has both indoor and garden seating. **Quinz** (✉ 29 N. Main St., ☎ 541/488–5937; $$) specializes in tapas-style portions of Italian, Greek, Spanish, and Middle Eastern food. For a light meal or some espresso, drop by the **Rogue Valley Roasting Co.** (✉ 917 E. Main St., ☎ 541/488–5902; $), a funky neighborhood hangout that's ideal for people-watching.

Any alternative-minded soul within a 100-mile radius of Ashland is likely to make the occasional trip to **Cork's Playbill Club**

(✉ 66 E. Main St., ☎ 541/488–2646), an infectious mixed gay/straight dance club and cocktail lounge with a restaurant and a stage for live performances. The Playbill Club, which got an early 1997 makeover, has been entertaining deviants for 100 years; ask to see the turn-of-the-century news clipping that warns persons of moral repute to avoid this scruffy pub. The crowd and staff here are extremely friendly.

## Sleeps

$$–$$$ 🏨 **Country Willows.** Dan Durant and David Newton bought this blue clapboard 1896 farmhouse-inn a few years ago. Guests here mingle with each other and the ducks, geese, goats, horses, and rabbits that roam about the 5 acres of willow trees. Such touches as twin-headed showers, wood-burning stoves, and fireplaces make for a romantic stay in the country. You won't find a nicer spot in Ashland. ✉ *1313 Clay St., Ashland, OR 97520,* ☎ *541/488–1590 or 800/945–5698,* FAX *541/488–1611. 9 rooms with phone and private bath. Pool, hot tub. Full breakfast. Mixed gay/straight.*

$$–$$$ 🏨 **Touvelle House.** Each room in Dennis and Carolee Casey's 1916 Craftsman inn has a distinct theme, such as the Prairie West suite, with wicker-and-pine furniture, a claw-foot tub, bear traps, and vintage photographs. Guests are free to wander the gardens and a small orchard. Touvelle House is in the historic community of Jacksonville, a short drive from Ashland. ✉ *455 N. Oregon St., Box 1891, Jacksonville, OR 97530,* ☎ *541/899–8938 or 800/846–8422,* FAX *541/899–3992. 6 rooms with phone and private bath. Pool, hot tub. Full breakfast. Mixed gay/straight.*

## At Your Fingertips

**Ashland Chamber of Commerce** (✉ 110 E. Main St., ☎ 541/482–3486).

# YACHATS, OREGON

Of the towns along Oregon's stunning coastline, mellow **Yachats** (pronounced Yah-hots) has the strongest following among lesbians and gays. There are few diversions other than the sound of the pounding surf and a famous spawning ground for smelt—so renowned that on the first weekend after July 4 hundreds gather for a pungent smelt-fry festival. From Yachats you're in a good position to explore 50 or 60 miles of the state's northern or southern coastline, where towns

range from several overrun with seaside kitsch to ones re-
splendent with natural beauty.

## Sleeps

For price ranges, *see* Chart B at the front of this guide. Artist
Susan Hovey built the **Morningstar Gallery** (⊠ Box 159,
Yachats 97498, ☎ 541/547–4412, FAX 541/547–4335; 3
rooms; $$–$$$) in 1995. She furnished the spectacular ocean-
front inn with a thoughtful blend of antiques and contemporary art. The **See Vue Motel** (⊠ 95590 Hwy. 101 S, Yachats
97498, ☎ 541/547–3227; 11 rooms; $) is your least-expensive
choice, a real bargain with some rooms for under $50 nightly
in season. The attractive but simple compound is perched on
a bluff overlooking the ocean. The **Yachats Inn** (⊠ 331 S. Coast
Hwy. 101, Box 307, Yachats 97498, ☎ 541/547–3456; 19
rooms; $–$$) is another solid option, with an indoor pool.
Seven of the rooms have fireplaces and kitchens.

In nearby Waldport, the **Cliff House** (⊠ Yaquina John Point,
Adahi Rd., Box 436, Waldport 97394, ☎ 541/563–2506;
4 rooms; $$–$$$$) has opulent antiques and potbellied
wood-burning stoves.

## At Your Fingertips

**Yachats Area Chamber of Commerce** (⊠ 441 Hwy. 101, Box
174, Yachats, OR 97498, ☎ 541/547–3530).

---

# TOFINO, BRITISH COLUMBIA

Hippies and environmentalists make up much of the popu-
lation of this peaceful, secluded town on the western shores
of Vancouver Island. Diversions include the **Pacific Rim Na-
tional Park,** which has three distinct sections, sandy **Long
Beach** (which is closest to Tofino), the **Broken Group Islands,**
and the **West Coast Trail.** Tofino is famous for bird-watching,
whale-watching, and its variety of art galleries and good
restaurants. For Eats and Sleeps price ranges, *see* Chart C at
the front of this guide. The **Alley Way Café** (⊠ Campbell and
1st Sts., ☎ 250/725–3105; $), open for breakfast and lunch,
specializes in healthful Mexican-influenced fare. The **Tofino
Co-Op** (⊠ 140 1st St., ☎ 250/725–3226) is a great place to
stock up on camping supplies or groceries, as well as fresh
baked goods.

### Sleeps

**$$** 🛏 **West Wind Guest House.** The cottage here sleeps up to six and has a full kitchen and a VCR with video library. The suite has a wet bar and a refrigerator. Both are filled with antiques and have goose-down duvets and feather beds. ⊠ *1321 Pacific Rim Hwy., Tofino, V0R 2Z0,* ☎ *250/725–2224,* ℻ *250/725–2212. 1 room and 1 cottage, each with TV and private bath. Hot tub, exercise room.*

### At Your Fingertips

**Tofino Travel InfoCentre** (⊠ 380 Campbell St., ☎ 250/725–3414).

# WHISTLER, BRITISH COLUMBIA

By train or car, it's only about two hours from downtown Vancouver to **Whistler,** one of North America's most challenging and beautiful ski resorts. In summer, this is also a fantastic place for hiking, climbing, cycling, and fishing. Both the drive and the ride via **B.C. Rail** (☎ 800/339–8752 in BC, 800/663–8238 elsewhere) are breathtaking.

Whistler's **Gay & Lesbian Ski Week** (for info: ⊠ 1238 Melville St., Suite 204, Vancouver, BC V6E 4N2, ☎ 604/688–5079 or 888/258–4883, ℻ 604/688–5033) was begun in 1992. At the time folks boycotting Colorado were seeking alternatives to Aspen's gay ski week. Held typically in early February, the weeklong Canadian get-together attracts sizeable crowds for 24 different events, including a pool party, a mountaintop tea dance, a picnic, and plenty of snowmobiling, skiing, and snowboarding at the first-rate Whistler Resort. For Sleeps price ranges, *see* Chart C at the front of this guide.

### Sleeps

**$** 🛏 **The Whistler Retreat.** This contemporary ski chalet nestled amid evergreens on the side of a mountain has a knock-out location, three friendly hosts (Brad, Andy, and Jim), and the ideal après-ski atmosphere, with a sauna, a hot tub, a pool table, a TV and VCR, and plenty of common space. The house is just a couple of miles from the slopes. The guys here will give you plenty of advice about what to do in the region. ⊠ *8561 Drifter Way, Whistler, BC V0N 1B8,* ☎ ℻ *604/938–9245. 3 rooms. Hot tub, exercise room. Full breakfast. Mostly mixed gay male/lesbian.*

# INDEX

Alabaster ✕, 65
Albion House 🏨, 84
Al Boccolino ✕, 11
Alexis Hotel 🏨, 28–29
Al Fresco ✕, 101–102
Allegro ✕, 70
Alton Baker Park, 145
Ambrosia ✕, 149
American Camp, 35
Anacortes, Washington, 38, 40, 46, 51, 52
Anne Hathaway's Cottage, 92
Art Gallery of Greater Victoria, 91
Artist's Studio Loft B&B 🏨, 32
Ashland, Oregon, 154–155

Back Hills 🏨, 107
Bacon Mansion 🏨, 31
Bandoleone ✕, 18
Basta's ✕, 123
Bay Cafe ✕, 43
Beaches
Portland, 137
Vancouver, 62
Beacon Hill Park, 91
Beetnix ✕, 72
Bellhouse Inn 🏨, 109–110
Benson Hotel 🏨, 138
Benton County Historical Museum, 146
Best Western New Oregon 🏨, 151
b. figueroa ✕, 11
Bilbo's ✕, 43
Bistro! Bistro! ✕, 68–69
Bizzarro Cafe ✕, 18, 20
B.J.'s (club), 104
Blitz-Weinhard Brewing Co., 117
Bloedel Conservatory, 62
Blue Ewe 🏨, 109
Bohematia ✕, 100–101
Boxx's/The Brig (club), 133
Bread and Ink Cafe ✕, 130

Bridgeport Brewing Co. ✕, 126
Bridges ✕, 73
Brite Spot ✕, 131
Broadway New American Grill ✕, 15
Buchan Hotel 🏨, 83
Bucky's Grill ✕, 43
Butchart Gardens, 92

Cactus ✕, 20
Cafe Arabesque ✕, 131
Café des Amis ✕, 123
Cafe Deux Soleil ✕, 76
Cafe Flora ✕, 20
Cafe Lago ✕, 18
Cafe Langley ✕, 46
Cafe Navarro ✕, 149
Cafe Olga ✕, 43
Cafe Zenon ✕, 149
Camille's ✕, 98
Campagne ✕, 11
Campbell House Inn 🏨, 152
Camping, 51–52
Canadian Craft Museum, 59
Capilano River Regional Park, 63
Capitol Hill Inn 🏨, 30–31
Caprial's Bistro and Wine ✕, 130
Carr House, 91
Caspian Mediterranean Cafe ✕, 149
Cassidy's ✕, 123
C.C. Attle's (club), 23
Celebrities (club), 78
Cemeteries, 92
Centennial Park, 93
Chambered Nautilus 🏨, 31
Changes (club), 23
Chez José ✕, 131
Chimera Gallery, 37
Choices (club), 136
Christina's ✕, 42
Christopher's ✕, 46
Church of Elvis, 117
CinCin ✕, 68

City Nightclub, *134*
Claddagh House ⌂, *107*
Club Arena/Pass the Pepper, *150*
Coastal Kitchen ✕, *15*
Coast Plaza at Stanley Park ⌂, *83*
Colibri B&B ⌂, *84*
Columbia Cottage ⌂, *85*
Conservatory (Seattle), *4*
Corvallis, Oregon, *146, 152*
Council Crest Park, *118*
Country Willows ⌂, *155*
Coupeville, Washington, *38–39, 46*
Courtyard Bistro ✕, *46*
Craigdarrouch Castle, *91*
Crescent Moon ✕, *103*
Crocodile ✕, *15*
Crow's Nest ⌂, *107*
Crow Valley Pottery, *37*
Crystal Garden Conservatory, *90–91*
Cuff (club), *23*
Cypress Falls Park, *63*

Dahlia Lounge, *11, 14*
Dan & Louis Oyster Bar ✕, *126–127*
Deception Pass State Park, *39*
Deer Harbor, Washington, *37*
Delilah's ✕, *69*
Denman Station (club), *78–79*
Denny-Blaine Park, *7–8*
Dick's Drive-in Restaurant ✕, *17*
Dilettante's ✕, *100*
Dr. Sun Yat-Sen Classical Chinese
  Garden, *60*
Doe Bay, Washington, *36*
Doe Valley Resort, *36*
Doll & Penny's ✕, *71*
Duck Soup ✕, *42*

Eagle (club)
*Portland, 134*
*Seattle, 23–24*
Eastsound, Washington, *36, 42–43*
Easy ✕, *16, 24*
El Gaucho ✕, *11*
Elysian Brewing Co. ✕, *15*
Embers (club), *134*

Encore (club), *24*
English Camp, *35*
Eugene, Oregon, *142–143*
  *bookstores, 152–153*
  *coffeehouse culture, 150*
  *exploring, 143–146*
  *festivals, 147*
  *guest houses, 151–152*
  *gyms, 153*
  *hotels, 151*
  *nightlife, 150–151*
  *phone numbers, 152*
  *publications, 152*
  *restaurants, 147–150*
  *transportation, 146–147*
Eugene Hilton ⌂, *151*
Excelsior Inn ⌂, *151–152*

Ferry service
  *Salt Spring Island, 97*
  *San Juan Islands, 39–40*
  *Victoria, 95–96*
Fidalgo Island, *38*
Fifth Avenue Suites ⌂, *138*
5 Spot Cafe ✕, *20*
Flying Fish ✕, *14*
Ford Centre for the Performing Arts,
  *59*
Forest Park, *118–119*
Ft. Casey State Park, *38*
Fountain Cafe ✕, *46*
Four Seasons ⌂, *82*
Friday Harbor, Washington, *35, 42,
  47, 48*
Friends ✕, *71*
Friends of Dorothy's ✕, *101*
Fulford Harbour, British Columbia,
  *94*
Fulford Inn ⌂, *109*
Funky Armadillo ✕, *73*

Gaches Mansion, *38*
Galiano Island, *95, 109–110*
Ganges Village, British Columbia, *93*
Garbanzo's ✕, *131*
Garden Path Cafe ✕, *42*

Gaslight Inn and Howell Street Suites
　🖭, *31*
Gastown Steam Clock, *60*
Genoa ✕, *127, 130*
Giorgina's ✕, *17*
Glenwood Cafe ✕, *149*
Glo's ✕, *17*
Good Chow ✕, *15*
Governor Hotel 🖭, *138*
Granville Island, *61*
Grasshopper ✕, *70*
Gravity Bar, *17*
Grayling Gallery, *37*
Green Lake, *9*
Green Rose 🖭, *108*
Grouse Mountain, *63*
Gypsy Cafe ✕, *126*

Hamburger Mary's ✕
*Portland, 126*
*Seattle, 17*
*Vancouver, 71*
Hastings House 🖭, *108*
Heathman Restaurant ✕, *122*
Hendricks Park, *145*
Herald Street Caffe ✕, *100*
Heritage House Hotel 🖭, *79*
Higgins ✕, *122*
Hill House 🖭, *31–32*
Hillside House 🖭, *48*
Hobo's ✕, *123, 134*
Holladay House B&B 🖭, *140*
Holland House Inn 🖭, *106*
Hopscotch ✕, *16*
Hopvine Pub, *16*
Hotel Dufferin (club), *79*
Hotel Vancouver 🖭, *82–83*
Hotel Vintage Park 🖭, *29*
Hotel Vintage Plaza 🖭, *138–139*
House Piccolo ✕, *101*
Hult Center for the Performing Arts,
　*144*

Il Piatto ✕, *130*
Imperial Hotel 🖭, *139*
Index, Washington, *32*

Indigo ✕, *69*
Inn at Swifts Bay 🖭, *49–50*
Inn at the Market 🖭, *29–30*
International Rose Test Garden, *118*
Island County Historical Museum,
　*38–39*

Jack's Bistro ✕, *16*
James House 🖭, *50*
Japanese Garden, *118*
Johnson House B&B 🖭, *84–85*
Joq's (club), *136*
Juicy Lucy's ✕, *76*
Julia's ✕, *21*

Kangaroo House 🖭, *49*
Kaspar's ✕, *18*
Katrina's ✕, *42*
Kid Mohair (club), *24*
Kitto ✕, *17*

La Catalana ✕, *130*
La Chanterelle ✕, *147, 149*
La Conner, Washington, *38, 40, 47,*
　*51, 52*
La Grec ✕, *76*
Landes House 🖭, *32*
Landis Hotel 🖭, *83*
L & L Market ✕, *150*
Lane County Historical Museum, *144*
Langley, Washington, *38, 46, 51*
Le Gavroche ✕, *68*
Libraries, *59*
Liliget ✕, *68*
Lime Kiln Point State Park, *36*
Limelight ✕, *72*
Lola's ✕, *68*
Lookout at the Harbour Center, *59*
Lopez Farm Cottages 🖭, *50*
Lopez Island, *37, 43, 46, 49–50*
Lopez Island Soda Fountain, *43, 46*
Luxy Bistro ✕, *71*
Lynn Canyon, *63*

Machiavelli ✕, *15–16*
McKenzie River Valley, *145–146*

MacMaster House 🏨, *139–140*
Madison Park, *8*
Mae's Phinney Ridge Cafe ✕, *21*
Mallory Hotel 🏨, *139*
Maple Leaf Grill ✕, *20*
Marilyn Moyer Chapel, *119*
Marina ✕, *100*
Mark Spencer Hotel 🏨, *139*
Mars (club), *79*
Mayne Island, *95, 110*
Meerkerk Rhododendron Gardens, *38*
Mekala's ✕, *149*
Mescalero ✕, *69*
Milestones ✕, *100*
Mr. Paddywack's (club), *24*
Moby's ✕, *102*
Montage ✕, *130*
Moonshadows Guest House 🏨, *110*
Moran State Park, *36*
Motel 6 🏨, *139*
Mt. Constitution, *36*
Mt. Maxwell, *94*
Mt. Parke, *95*
Mt. Pisgah Arboretum, *145*
Mt. Tuam, *94*
Ms. T's (club), *79–80*
Museum of Natural
   History–University of Oregon, *144*
Museum of Northwest Art, *38*

Naam ✕, *76*
Neighbours (club), *24–25*
Nelson House 🏨, *85*
Nitobe Memorial Garden, *62*
Noodle Studio ✕, *16*
Numbers (club), *80*

Oak Bay, British Columbia, *92, 111*
Oak Bay Guest House 🏨, *106*
Oak Harbor, Washington, *39*
O'Canada House 🏨, *84*
Odlin County Park, *37*
Odyssey (club), *80*
Odyssey Contemporary Maritime
   Museum, *5*
Old Wives' Tales ✕, *131–132*

Olga, Washington, *43*
Olympic Lights 🏨, *48*
Orcas Island, *36–37, 41, 49*
Oregon Convention Center, *119*
Oregon Historical Center, *116*
Oregon Maritime Museum, *115*
Oregon Museum of Science and
   Industry, *115*
Oregon State University, *146*
O-Tooz, An Energie Bar ✕, *72*
Owen Rose Garden, *143*

Pacific Science Center, *7*
Painted Table ✕, *14*
Palace ✕, *14*
Palmer's ✕, *47*
Panorama (club), *134–135*
Papa Haydn ✕, *123*
Paramount Hotel 🏨, *29*
Parkhill Hotel 🏨, *83*
Parliament Buildings, *90*
Penny Farthing 🏨, *85*
Philadelphia Fevre ✕, *21*
Pike Place Market, *4–5*
Pittock Mansion, *118*
Pizzacato ✕, *127*
Pluto's ✕, *100*
Point Ellice House ✕, *98*
Ponti Seafood Grill ✕, *18*
Portland, Oregon, *112–114*
   bookstores, *141*
   Chinatown, *117*
   coffeehouse culture, *132*
   Downtown, *114–116*
   exploring, *114–120*
   festivals, *121*
   Glazed Terra-Cotta Historic District,
      *116*
   guest houses, *139–140*
   gyms, *141*
   Hawthorne District, *119–120*
   hotels, *138–139*
   Lloyd District, *119*
   nightlife, *133–136*
   Northeast Broadway, *119*
   Northwest, *117*

Old Town, 117
Pearl District, 116
phone numbers, 140
publications, 140
restaurants, 121–123, 128–132
sex clubs and bathhouses, 137
Skidmore Historic District, 117
Southwest, 118–119
Stark Street, 116–117
transportation, 120–121
Yamhill Historic District, 115
**Portland Art Museum,** 116
**Portland Center for the Performing Arts,** 116
**Portland State University,** 116
**Port Townsend, Washington,** 39, 40, 46, 47, 50
**Prow** ✕, 69
**Purple Parrot** ✕, 102

**Quattro on Fourth** ✕, 72–73
**Queen City Grill** ✕, 11
**Queen Elizabeth Park,** 62

**Raincity Grill** ✕, 69–70
**Raintree** ✕, 70
**Ravenscroft Inn** ⬚, 50
**Re-bar** (club), 25
**ReeBar** (club), 101
**RiverPlace Promenade,** 115
**Rooster Rock State Park,** 137
**Rose Garden Arena,** 119
**Ross Bay Cemetery,** 92
**Rover's** ✕, 18
**Roxy** ✕, 127
**Royal British Columbia Museum,** 90
**Royal Empress Hotel** ⬚, 106
**Royal Hotel Pub,** 80
**Royal London Wax Museum,** 90
**R Place** (club), 25
**Ruckle Provincial Park,** 94
**Rumors** (club), 104
**Rural Roots B&B** ⬚, 85–86

**Saigon Kitchen** ✕, 132
**Salal Cafe** ✕, 46

**Sala Thai** ✕, 73
**Salem, Oregon,** 120, 137
**Salisbury House** ⬚, 31
**Salt Spring Island,** 88–89
bookstores, 111
coffeehouse culture, 103–104
exploring, 93–94
guest houses, 107–109
nightlife, 104–105
phone numbers, 110
publications, 110
restaurants, 101–103
transportation, 97
weather, 98
**San Juan Island,** 35–36, 42, 47, 48, 52
**San Juan Island National Historic Park,** 35
**San Juan Islands,** 34
camping, 51–52
coffeehouse culture, 47
exploring, 34–39
guest houses, 47–51
nightlife, 47
phone numbers, 52
publications, 52
restaurants, 41–47
transportation, 39–41
weather, 41
**Santa Fe Burrito Company** ✕, 150
**Sauce Box** ✕, 126
**Sauvies Island,** 137
**Scandals** (club), 135
**Seattle, Washington,** 1–3
Belltown, 6
bookstores, 33
Capitol Hill, 3–4, 15–18
coffeehouse culture, 21–22
Downtown, 4–5, 11, 14–15
exploring, 3–9
festivals, 10
guest houses, 30–32
gyms, 33
hotels, 28–30
International District, 6
Lake Washington shoreline, 7–8

music clubs, 27
nightlife, 22–28
phone numbers, 32–33
Pioneer Square, 5–6
publications, 33
Queen Anne Hill, 7
restaurants, 10–21
Seattle Center, 7
sex clubs and bathhouses, 28
transportation, 9–10
University District, Wallingford, and
    Freemont, 8–9
Volunteer Park, 4
weather, 10
**Seattle Aquarium,** 5
**Seattle Art Museum,** 5
**Seattle Asian Art Museum,** 4
**Seattle International Film Festival,** 10
**Seattle Rose Garden,** 9
**Shaker's** ✕, 127
**Shamrock Motel** ⊞, 106
Shaw Island, 37
**Sheraton Hotel & Towers** ⊞, 29
**Ship Bay Oyster House** ✕, 43
**Siam on Broadway** ✕, 16–17
Sidney, British Columbia, 92–93
**Silverado** (club), 135
**Simpatico Bistro** ✕, 20
**66 Motel** ⊞, 151
**Skagit County Historical Museum,** 38
**Skidmore Fountain,** 117
**Skinner Butte Park,** 143
**Sneakers** (club), 137
**Sophie's Cosmic Cafe** ✕, 73
**Sorrento** ⊞, 29
**Southern Gulf Islands,** 94–95
**Space Needle,** 7
**Spencer Butte,** 145
**Spinnakers** ✕, 100
**Spring Bay** ⊞, 49
**Springfield, Oregon,** 145, 151, 152
**Springtree Cafe** ✕, 42
**Steamworks** ✕, 70–71
**Stepho's** ✕, 71
**Still Life** ✕, 21
**Sullivan's Gulch B&B** ⊞, 140

**Summerhill** ⊞, 108
**Sunny Side Up** ⊞, 109
**Suriya Thai Cuisine** ✕, 127
**Sutton Place Hotel** ⊞, 82
**Swans Hotel** ⊞, 106
**Sylvia Hotel** ⊞, 83
**Szechuan Chongqing** ✕, 73

**Tacoma, Washington,** 27–28
**Taiko** ✕, 71
**Theater**
Portland, 120
Seattle, 7
**Theater buildings**
Eugene, 144
Portland, 116
Vancouver, 59
**Thumpers** (club), 25–26
**Timberline Tavern,** 26
**Tio Pepe's** ✕, 73
**Tofino, British Columbia,** 156–157
**Tojo's** ✕, 72
**Tomato Fresh Food** ✕, 76
**Tom McCall Waterfront Park,** 115
**Touvelle House** ⊞, 155
**Trattoria Mitchelli** ✕, 15
**Trumpeter Inn** ⊞, 48
**28 East** ✕, 130

**UBC Botanical Garden,** 62
**UBC Museum of Anthropology,** 62
**Underground Seattle,** 6
**Union Bay Cafe** ✕, 20
**University Inn** ⊞, 30
**University of British Columbia (UBC),**
    62
**University of Oregon,** 144–145
**University of Washington,** 8, 23
**University of Washington Park**
    **Arboretum,** 8
**Uwajimaya** (department store), 6

**Vancouver, British Columbia,** 53–56
bookstores, 86–87
Chinatown, 60
coffeehouse culture, 76–77

Commercial Drive, 60
Downtown, 58–59, 65, 68–72
exploring, 56–63
festivals, 64
Gastown, 59–60, 65, 68–72
guest houses, 84–86
gyms, 87
hotels, 81–83
Kitsilano, 61
nightlife, 77–81
North Shore, 62–63
phone numbers, 86
publications, 86
restaurants, 64–76
sex clubs and bathhouses, 81
Stanley Park, 58
transportation, 63–64
West End, 57–58, 65, 68–72
West Side, 60–62
Yaletown, 58
Vancouver, Washington, 136–137
Vancouver Art Gallery, 59
Vancouver Maritime Museum, 61
Vancouver Museum, 61
Vancouver Public Aquarium, 58
Vancouver Public Library, 59
Vandusen Botanical Garden, 62
Vanier Park, 61
Vashon Island, 32
Vesuvius, British Columbia, 94
Vesuvius Neighborhood Pub, 103
Victoria, British Columbia, 88–89
bookstores, 110–111
coffeehouse culture, 103
exploring, 89–92
festivals, 98
guest houses, 106–107
gyms, 111
hotels, 106
nightlife, 104
phone numbers, 110
publications, 110
restaurants, 98–101

sex clubs and bathhouses, 105
transportation, 95–97
weather, 98
Victoria Butterfly Gardens, 92
Villa Valmont ☒, 108–109

Washington Park, 118
Waterfront Centre ☒, 82
Weekender ☒, 106–107
WestCoast Camlin ☒, 30
WestCoast Plaza Park Suites ☒, 30
WestCoast Roosevelt Hotel ☒, 30
WestCoast Vance ☒, 30
Westcott Bay Sea Farm, 36
West End Guest House ☒, 84
West Sound, Washington, 37
West Wind Guest House ☒, 157
Whale Museum, 36
Whale-watching, 36
Whidbey Inn, 51
Whidbey Island, 38–39, 40, 46, 51, 52
Whistler, British Columbia, 157
Whistler Retreat ☒, 157
White Swan ☒, 51
Wild Abandon ✕, 131
Wild Ginger ✕, 14
Wild Lily Ranch B&B ☒, 32
Wildrose ✕, 17–18, 26
Wildwood ✕, 122–123
Windsong ☒, 49
Woodland Park, 9
World Forestry Center, 118
Wreck Beach, 62

Yachats, Oregon, 155–156

Zasu ✕, 14
Zefiro's ✕, 123, 126
Zoos
Portland, 118
Seattle, 9